Marc Quinn h

steidl MACK

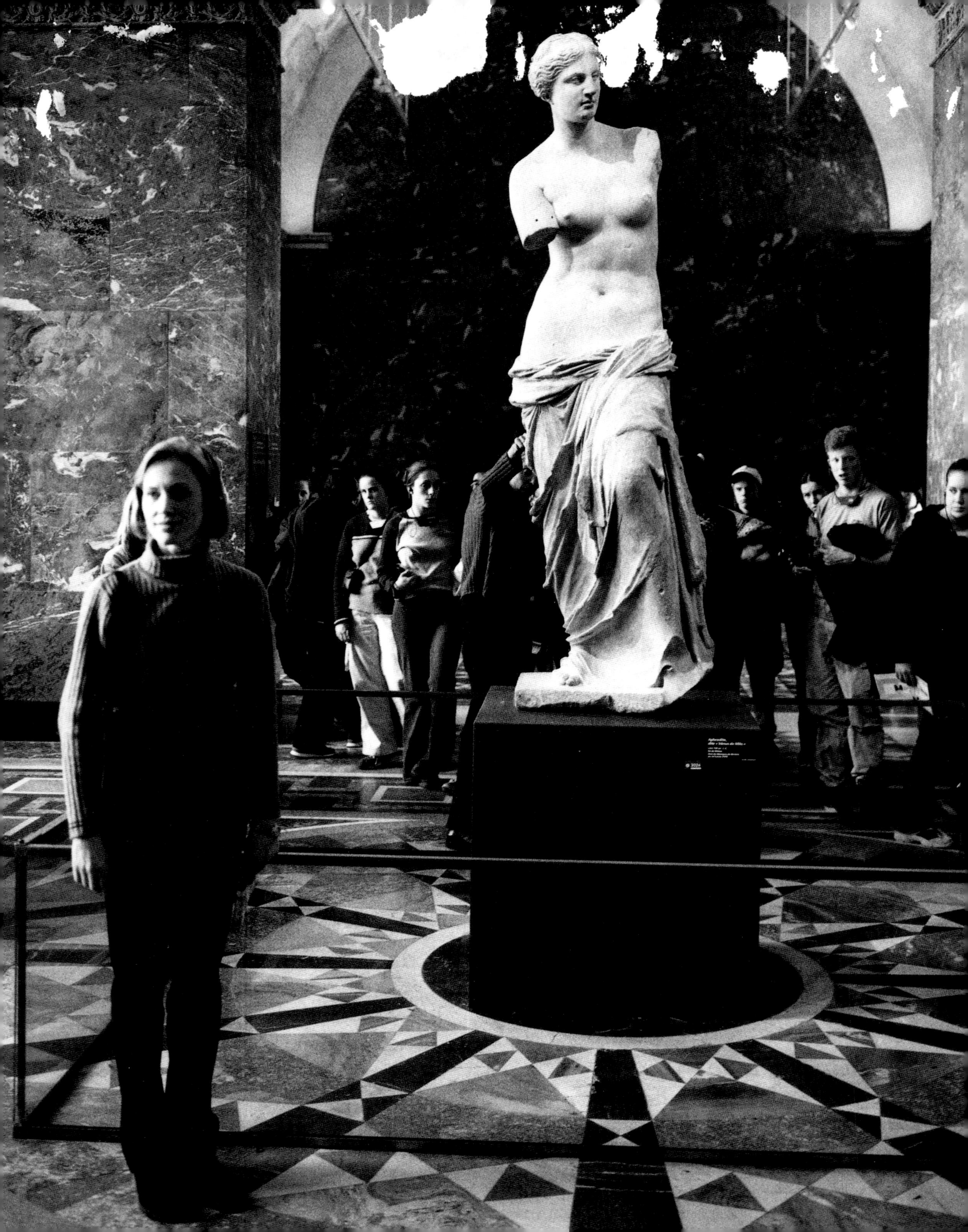
Aphrodite,
dite « Vénus de Milo »
3024

Marc Quinn
Alison Lapper Pregnant, 2005
The Fourth Plinth, Trafalgar Square, London

The sculpture Alison Lapper Pregnant is the culmination of a body of work begun by Marc Quinn in the late 1990s. 'I was walking around the British Museum and the Louvre noticing how the crowds admired the fragmented classical statuary. For example, the *Venus de Milo* is a cultural short-hand for feminine beauty, and I thought that if someone whose real body was that shape came into the room the same people would probably react in a completely opposite manner. That gap between Art and Life, what is acceptable in art and unacceptable in life, seemed like an interesting area to explore. I decided to make a marble portrait of a real person whose body was of a similar form, but obviously they were not a fragment but a whole person'. The first sitter for the artist was Peter Hull, a Paralympic athlete who won a gold medal for swimming at the Paralympics. He was born with no legs, significantly shortened arms, and no hands. Quinn then went on to make a series of eight marble portraits of 'subjects with similar bodies.' The complete suite of works were initially shown at the Prada Foundation in Milan in 2000, followed by the Victoria & Albert Museum in London in 2001, where they were mixed with the neo-classical sculptures in the museum's collection, such as Canova's *Three Graces*.

'When I made the portraits I realised that part of the work was about what we see as beautiful. Disabled bodies are hardly represented in the history of art and when they are, they are usually interpreted as something 'other' or negative. To see these different bodies reproduced in the material of beauty and heroism, marble, involved a celebration of a wider notion of beauty and humanity.'

After the initial eight sculptures, the artist made a portrait of Alison Lapper when she was eight months pregnant. A year or so later he made another portrait of Alison with her son, Parys, on her knee. They were shown at the White Cube gallery in London in December 2000.

'When I was making these sculptures, one of the things which I kept feeling was that they were like sculpture, especially public sculpture, from the future. When the Fourth Plinth competition came along in 2003 it seemed one of these pieces would be the right thing to enter. I looked at Trafalgar Square and I realised that whilst Nelson himself had lost an arm and his sight in one eye, he was never thought of as disabled and it seemed relevant to reanimate this dormant aspect of the square. Most public monumental sculpture in Trafalgar Square is celebrating dead, male military heroes, and Alison seemed to me to be the opposite. The other sculptures commemorate an event that has happened, they commemorate the past, but Alison is pregnant in the sculpture, and for me, she commemorates the future potential of humanity, possibility and hope. I also felt that motherhood was an ignored achievement in general, in terms of public art.'

The artist was among 120 artists asked to submit a proposal. He was then shortlisted and asked to create a maquette in March 2004 and won the competition.

The sculpture took over a year to make, three months to find the right piece of stone then ten months of carving. The sculpture was carved in the same way in which marble sculpture has been carved since antiquity. The model, in this case the life cast of Alison, is carefully marked with hundreds of pencil dots which serve as reference points and annotations for changes which the artist requires. Using a compass and a pointing device, the distance between the dots is increased and the new measurements transferred to the new block of stone. After a period of months the result is a copy of the model with an outer layer of about 2 cm of stone. At this point the artist and the stonemasons work more closely together and using photography and drawings create the final surface of the work.

The sculpture was finally installed on the plinth on 15 September, 2005.

…g prepares you for the impact of Marc Quinn's extraordinary sculpture *Alison Lapper Pregnant*. The luminosity of the white marble flares like a torch against the gray backdrop of the National Gallery, and her head, huge and authoritative, determinedly turned away, holds its place with the spire of St Martins in the Field, the dome of the National Gallery, and Nelson's Column.

Sculpture is a public art and this sculpture, in a square that was once the heart of the British Empire, and is today the meeting place for all of London, has a constantly changing dialogue with the viewer.

Approaching the sculpture from behind across the newly pedestrianised expanse you are stunned by the epic size of the figure. Standing underneath her, all that is actually visible is a slice of her head with sternly cropped hair, and broad forehead of almost ancient nobility.

But then, back away, and the proud soldier disappears and you see the voluptuously pregnant torso of a naked, vulnerable woman.

A few steps later the absent arms are glimpsed – yet this is not a sculpture of a disabled person, but of a proud Helenic warrior. The very absence of limbs allows us to focus on the beauty of her head and torso.

The power of the sculpture lies in the fact that both these impressions – ancient and modern, mythical and realistic – continue after the initial surprise to exist in tandem, resulting in a wonderful series of paradoxes. The dialogue of opposites also exists, crucially, between the sculpture and the square. The other figures are statesmen, generals, clothed in the regalia of their public personae and status: this is the only female, the only nude, the only figure left unadorned.

Quite simply, the beauty of this work of art exists on its own terms, and apart from the numberless moral conclusions which can be drawn from it. Its very limbless simplicity, concentrating the energy into the centre of the figure, reduces the form to its essence; the play of light and shadow on this mass, with its luminous weight, its quiet strength, makes the ordinary subject extraordinary.

It is my belief that this great public sculpture should stand permanently in a major public space. It should stay in Trafalgar Square.

Richard Rogers

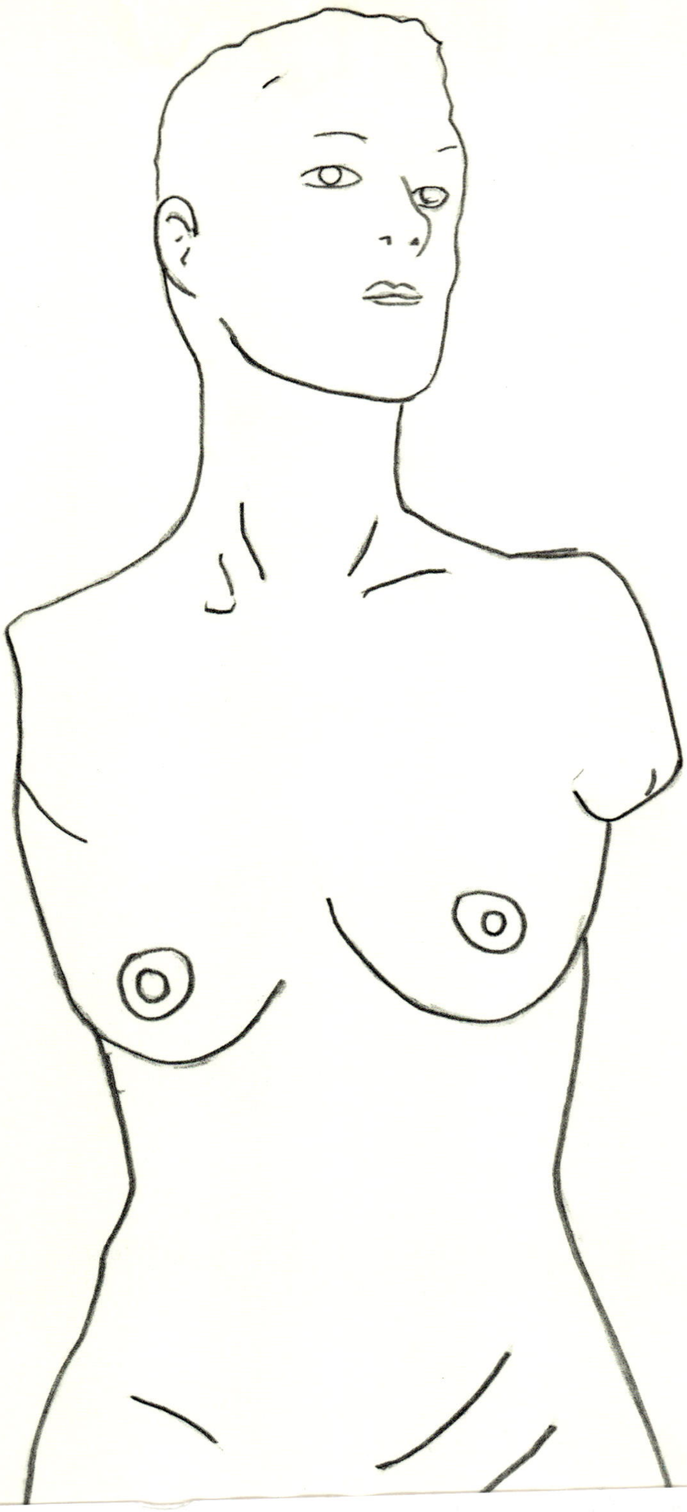

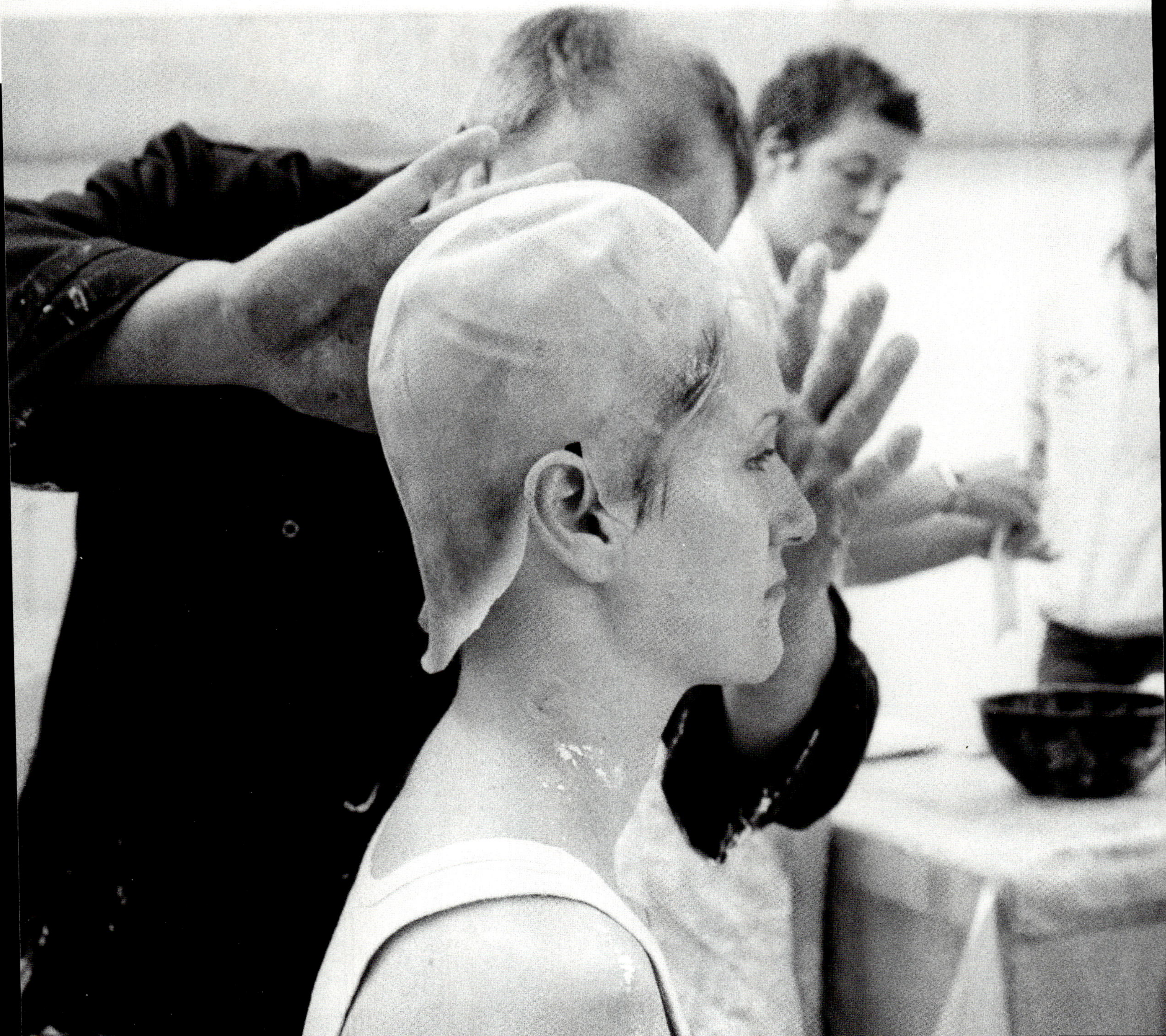

Pregnant, armless... and going on display in London

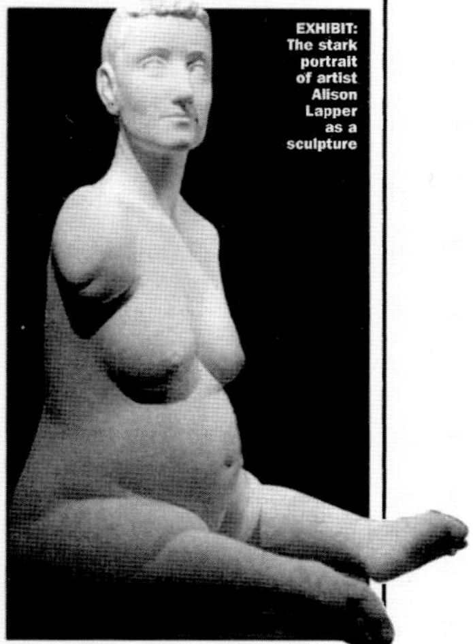

EXHIBIT: The stark portrait of artist Alison Lapper as a sculpture

Shocking new statue for Trafalgar Square

By **Maurice Mcleod**

A STATUE of an armless, naked, pregnant woman is to fill the famously-empty fourth plinth below Lord Nelson's Column in Trafalgar Square.

The controversial work by British artist Marc Quinn will be displayed for at least a year from spring 2005 at the historic central London site.

Speaking after the announcement at City Hall yesterday, Mr Quinn, 40, from London, said: "I was surprised but I am thrilled to win the competition."

Mr Quinn, who once made a refrigerated cast of his head using nine pints of his own blood, said he hoped his work would introduce some femininity to the square. The statue is a portrait of his friend, disabled artist Alison Lapper, when she was eight-and-a-half months pregnant. It will be carved out of one block of white marble and will stand 15ft high.

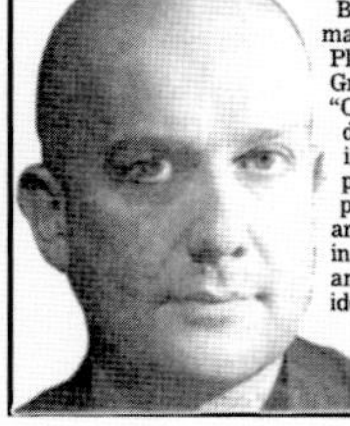

WINNER: Marc Quinn

Bert Massie, chairman of the Fourth Plinth Commissioning Group, said last night: "Congratulations are due to Marc for realising that disabled people's bodies have a power and beauty that are rarely recognised in an age where youth and 'perfection' are idolised."

Trafalgar tribute

I congratulate the decision to display Marc Quinn's sculpture Alison Lapper Pregnant in Trafalgar Square (Report, March 16). This selection displays a willingness to promote the marvellous diversity in our society and by doing so is embracing the notion of equality. The sculpture has also uncovered the attitudes of society that pregnant disabled women are shocking. What actually seems shocking are the negative and damaging attitudes it provokes.

Andrew Crooks
Campaigns officer, Scope

● Great to read Alison Lapper's statue will adorn the empty plinth in Trafalgar Square, but bad to read your standfirst describing it as a tribute to a "thalidomide victim". Anyone who watched Ms Lapper with her son, Parys, in the BBC's Child of Our Time series will know she's most certainly no victim.

Gill Hitchcock
London

Yes, she is a truly courageous woman. But the home of Nelson is no place for this statue

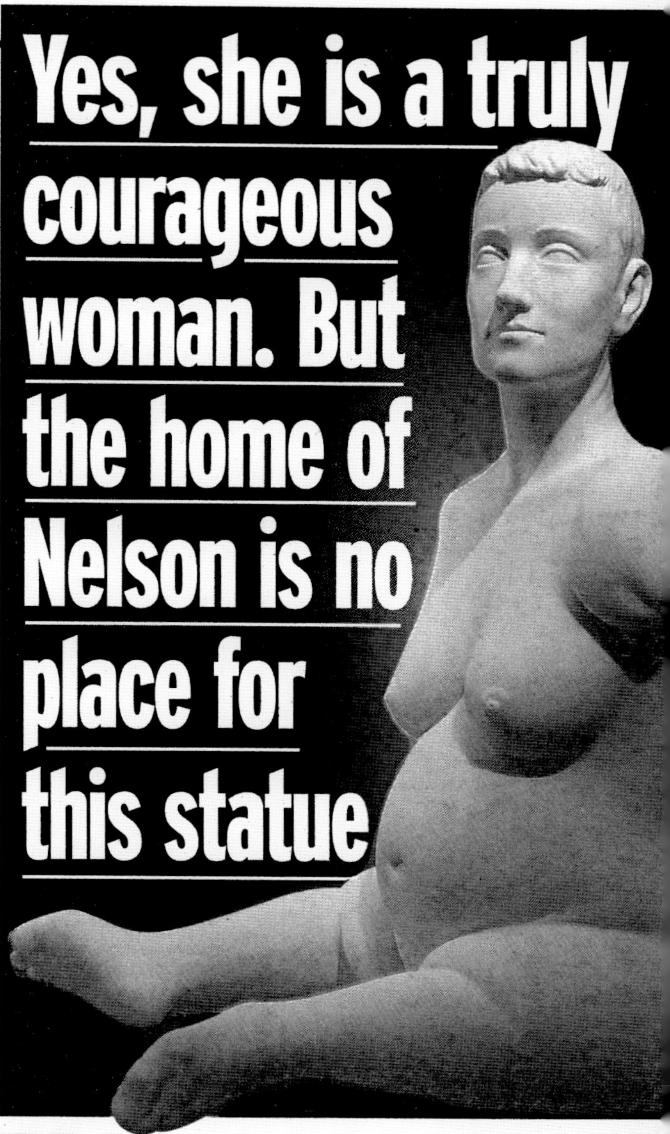

FOR Alison Lapper — the model and inspiration for the statue which, for the next 15 months, will occupy the fourth plinth in London's Trafalgar Square — I have nothing but admiration.

Ms Lapper — disabled by thalidomide and shown gloriously pregnant — is a friend of Marc Quinn, the sculptor who submitted the nude figure to the committee which chooses the works of art to go on display in the shadow of Nelson's Column.

If, as I suspect, Mr Quinn thought of his work as a celebration of both courage and motherhood, I have no doubt that he is right. The manner in which Ms Lapper has overcome her disability and is bringing up her four-year-old son is only to be admired.

But Alison Lapper Pregnant, as the sculpture is called, is the wrong statue in the wrong place. Trafalgar Square ought to immortalise the great moments in our history.

That, I believe, requires the removal of some of the rubbish on which the pigeons now perch, but it makes it a wholly inappropriate site and setting for both the naked mother-to-be and for another work, an extraordinary conglomeration of sticks and wire — called Hotel For Birds — which is to follow it.

The absurdity of the enterprise is illustrated by Mr Quinn's complaint that Nelson's Column is 'the epitome of a phallic male monument' — a piece of sub-Freudian nonsense which will leave most Londoners and visitors to the capital absolutely bewildered.

Nelson happens to be the authentic hero of English history, the sailor who died at the moment of victory in the battle that established this nation's maritime supremacy and kept us safe from invasion for 200 years.

If he is not entitled to be immortalised in stone, who is?

The answer to that question is clear. The too-often empty plinth should be permanently occupied by a statue of William Shakespeare — whose genius set Britain and the English language apart from the rest of the world.

There is a second-rate bust of him in Leicester Square but the city that first produced his plays and still thrives on his reputation lacks a decent memorial to the man rightly described by Ben Jonson as 'not of an age, but for all time'.

So, Mr Quinn thinks that Trafalgar Square needs some femininity — and I think it needs William Shakespeare.

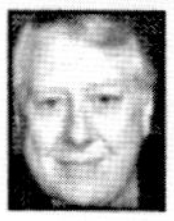

by **Roy Hattersley**

BERT MASSIE, chairman of the Disability Rights Commission, has congratulated Mr Quinn on recognising that 'disabled bodies have a power and beauty which is rarely recognised'.

I think that praise is well-deserved. I go further. Pregnancy is, or ought to be, a joy which has an equal or even greater beauty.

I would be delighted to see Alison Lapper Pregnant in the Tate Modern — perhaps side by side with Hotel For Birds.

But Trafalgar Square ought to remind Londoners and tourists alike about the glories of our history, courage and sacrifice or great vision that changed lives and futures for the better rather than personal courage, however awe-inspiring that might be.

And do not let either Mr Quinn or Mr Massie suggest that I want to hide the part that has been played in our island's story by the disabled and the disadvantaged.

I am emphatically not one of the people who believe that handicap should be shut out from public view — although I recognise that anyone who criticises the choice of the Quinn sculpture will be accused of that offence.

Those who believe that my objection is to the state offering a proper tribute to the handicapped ought to be reminded that Admiral Lord Nelson lost an eye and an arm in his country's service.

Had he not believed that his destiny was to save Britain from Napoleon, he might have retired to restful ease ashore.

So all the nonsense about 'phallic' images aside, Trafalgar Square is already a genuine tribute to the way in which the disabled can transcend their handicaps.

Of course, the committee that chose the Alison Lapper sculpture will be abused for the crime of 'political correctness'.

There is much to be said for what is sometimes called political correctness when it condemns racist abuse, rejects the humiliation of gays and stands out against the denigration of women.

But the Trafalgar Square decision is simply old-fashioned foolishness — the absolute inability to judge what is fitting and appropriate and what is not. It really *is* political correctness gone mad.

I can hear the cultural avant garde already demanding to know what their critics think about some of the other statues which decorate Trafalgar Square. My answer is clear. I do not regard most of them as remotely appropriate to the showpiece of the nation.

General Sir Charles Napier, for example — whose claim to fame was slaughtering his way to victory in the Indian province of Sind — is said to be the author of one of the most spectacular bad taste jokes in our history.

SURROUNDED by the dead and the dying, he sent back to Whitehall the simple Latin verb 'Peccavi' — 'I have sinned'. I would certainly like to see him thrown out of Trafalgar Square.

What the public wants in Trafalgar Square is — or ought to be — important. This hub of British civilisation should celebrate individual examples of national achievement and British greatness.

Alongside Shakespeare I would nominate Milton for literature, Turner and Constable for painting, Elgar for music,
Newton and Rutherford f
science, Wren and Hawksmo
for architecture.

I doubt if one Londoner —
Briton — in 100 wants Alis
Lapper Pregnant to decora
the empty plinth. And it is t
selection committee's attitu
to that which causes me t
most offence.

The choice of the pregna
and disabled nude figure loo
suspiciously like an attempt
teach the uneducated a
unenlightened masses a less
in sensitivity and sophisticati

It reminds me of tho
examples of 'proletarian re
ism' of the old Soviet Union
absolutely nothing to do wi
art and everything to do wi
propaganda.

If Mr Quinn and the selecti
committee think this coun
needs propaganda on behalf
the disabled, it does the peo
of Britain a gross disservice.

Most of us will share the vi
that Alison Lapper is somec
to admire — a person not
hide or to ignore but to ce
brate. But we do object to t
suggestion that we have to
taught about the disabled a
that our lack of understandi
and feeling has to be ramm
down our throats.

There are dozens of wa
that can be done. And the
are thousands of opportunit
to express our admiration
people who battle their w
against disadvantages.

But the simple truth is th
Trafalgar Square is meant
something else.

The new star of Trafalgar Square...a disabled nude who is 8½ months' pregnant

By **Tim Hall**

A 15FT pregnant disabled nude is to sit alongside military heroes and royalty in Trafalgar Square.

Alison Lapper Pregnant, a white marble sculpture by contemporary artist Marc Quinn, has been chosen to occupy the empty fourth plinth at one of Britain's most famous landmarks.

The artist said he hoped his work would introduce some femininity to the square and would represent a new model of female heroism.

But the choice was greeted with ridicule by art critics and politicians, mindful of the strong public backing there has been for a statue of the Queen Mother on the plinth.

The other platforms in Trafalgar Square are occupied by George IV, Sir Charles Napier and Major General Sir Henry Havelock.

Alison Lapper Pregnant, chosen by a team of contemporary art lovers selected by London mayor Ken Livingstone, will remain in place for 15 months, then be replaced by another modern work chosen by the same group, Hotel for the Birds, by German artist Thomas Schutte, which has been likened to a giant multicoloured Meccano set.

David Lee, editor of the art magazine The Jackdaw, described the winning sculptures as 'ghastly'. He said they were chosen by 'a conceptual art clique' and would appeal to only 'about half a dozen people' within it.

Robin Simon, editor of the British Art Journal, said he was 'infinitely depressed' by the choices, but added: 'Thankfully these sculptures are not going to be around for ever'.

Tory culture spokesman Julie Kirkbride said: 'The politically correct lobby has prevailed. Whilst childbirth is a great thing to celebrate, I still think we should have focused on individuals of great achievement the nation ought to commemorate.'

The Fourth Plinth Commissioning Group, made up of left-wing writers and broad-

'Powerful responses'

casters including Channel 4's Jon Snow, first selected a shortlist of six contemporary pieces, models of which were displayed at the National Gallery.

Public participation was invited through a Greater London Authority website and the group took the responses into consideration before choosing the winners.

Also in the final six were a Ford Fiesta splattered with pigeon droppings and two wooden lifesize replicas of Tomahawk cruise missiles.

A campaign led by the Daily Mail had revealed that a vast majority of people would have liked to have seen a statue of an iconic historical figure or role model, with the Queen Mother the favourite.

But the FPCG dismissed the idea from the beginning.

The group is chaired by Sandy Nairne, director of the National Portrait Gallery and a Channel 4 filmmaker.

He said: 'Both of these proposals have extraordinary artistic value and merit.

'Though they could not be more different from each other, both works will encourage powerful responses from Londoners and visitors and will enhance London's reputation as a leader in the visual arts.'

The GLA admitted that many of the people who voted on its website had been against the idea of contemporary art in Trafalgar Square.

But it said Quinn's statue 'considered questions of idealism, heroism, femininity, prejudice and identity'.

Londoner Quinn, 40, said: 'I was surprised because you never know what's going to happen in a competition, but I am thrilled.'

The statue is a portrait of his friend, disabled artist Alison Lapper, when she was eight-and-a-half months pregnant.

He said he deliberately chose a subject matter far removed from the military heroes that are frequently displayed in public squares.

'Nelson's Column is the epitome of a phallic male monument and I felt that the square needed some femininity, linking Boudicca near the Houses of Parliament,' he said.

The choice was welcomed by the Disability Rights Commission. Chairman Bert Massie said: 'I'm extremely proud that one of the most popular tourist attractions in London will display a very powerful sculpture of a disabled woman.

'Congratulations to Marc for realising that disabled bodies have a power and beauty rarely recognised in an age where youth and "perfection" are idolised.'

The plinth was erected in 1841 to accommodate a statue of King William IV on horseback, but it was never cast because funds ran out.

When the two statues have had their 15-month runs, the competition will be restaged.

t.hall@dailymail.co.uk

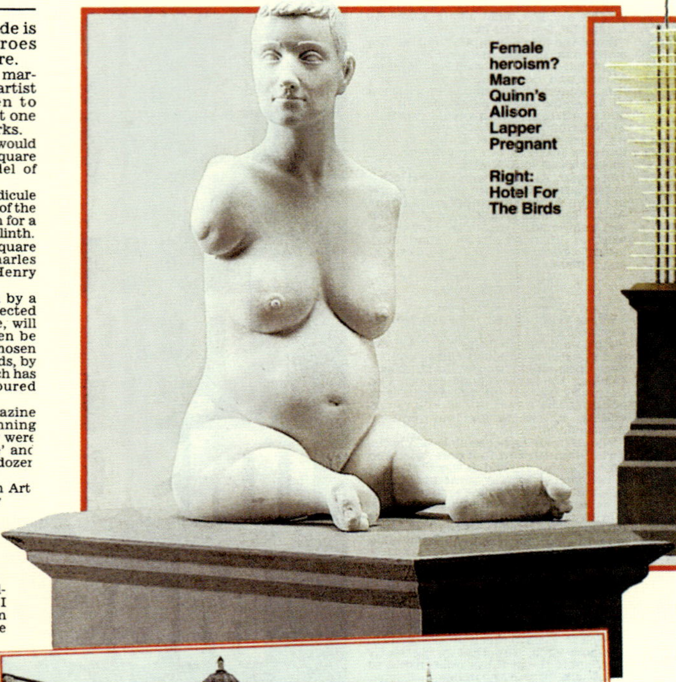

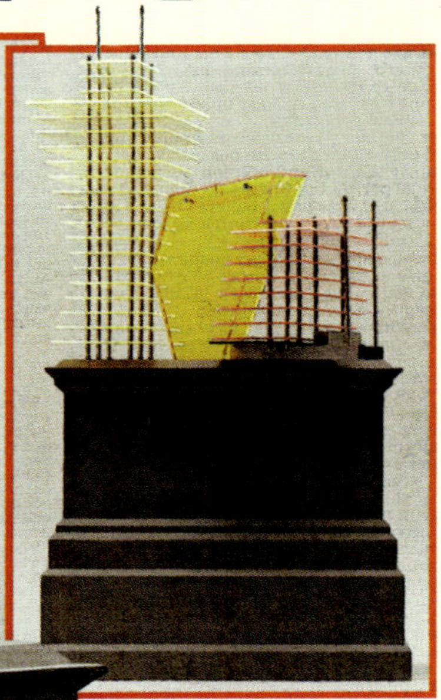

Female heroism? Marc Quinn's Alison Lapper Pregnant

Right: Hotel For The Birds

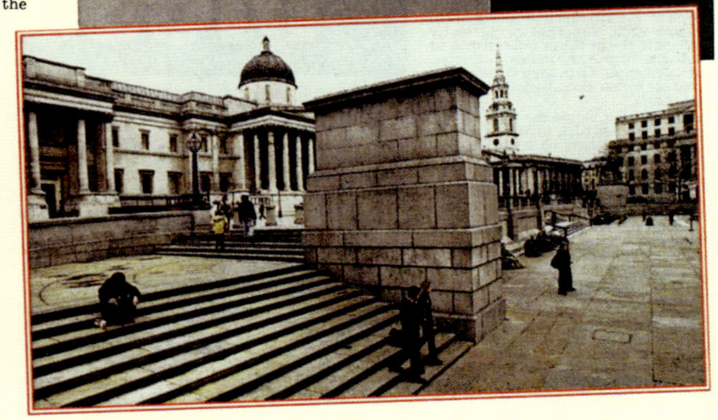

Place of honour: The empty Trafalgar Square plinth where the works will be displayed

Marc Quinn — Alison Lapper Pregnant

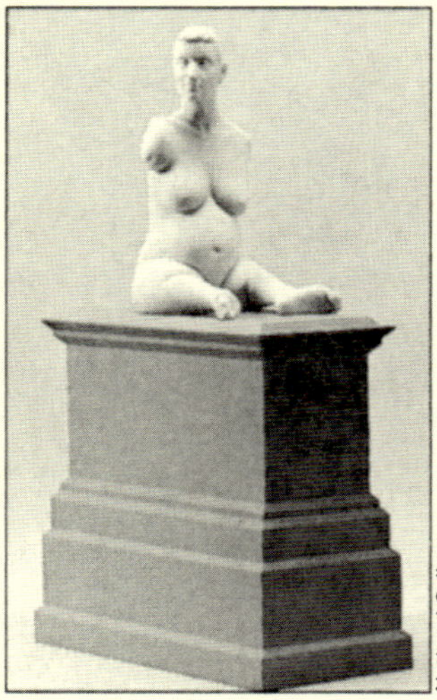

National Gallery

ONE of the superficially more cerebral YBAs, Quinn, 39, creates sculptures that tackle philosophical and scientific issues. Technology is often crucial to the form of his work, as in his DNA portrait of the scientist John Sulston or his notorious Self, a bust of himself made from nine pints of his own blood, frozen and constantly refrigerated.

His entry is an enlarged version of one of his recent series of marble sculptures of disabled people. "In the past, heroes such as Nelson conquered the outside world," he says. "Now it seems to me they conquer their own circumstances and the prejudices of others."

Probably true, but Quinn's noble sentiments are evidently also infused with the equally ignoble desire to shock.

March 2004:
Media response to the selection of
Quinn's proposal for the Fourth Plinth

Evening Standard Tuesday, 16 March 2004 3

AS MAYOR'S COMMITTEE DECIDES WHAT GOES ON THE TRAFALGAR SQUARE PLINTH

Art world divided by marble disabled nude

By Luke Leitch
Arts Reporter

CONTROVERSY was today raging over the art works that have finally been chosen to occupy the empty fourth plinth in Trafalgar Square.

A white marble sculpture by Marc Quinn of disabled artist Alison Lapper, when she was eight months pregnant, and another modernist concept called Hotel For The Birds, by German artist Thomas Schütte — drew equal measures of contempt and praise when Mayor Ken Livingstone's Four Plinth Commissioning Committee announced the winners today.

Quinn's Alison Lapper Pregnant will rest on the plinth for 18 months from next spring, to be replaced after that by Schütte's Perspex work. He intended the image to counterbalance the heavy presence of military images in statues across London.

But there was vociferous condemnation of the verdicts by the committee of art lovers, chaired by National Portrait director Sandy Nairne and including Channel 4 news anchorman Jon Snow, Lazards merchant banker Diane Henry and disability adviser Richard Reiser.

The Evening Standard's art critic Brian Sewell damned the decision, saying: "I dislike the Quinn intensely and I can see no virtue in the Schütte. It's a gloriously fudged decision and they better try and get it right next time."

David Lee, editor of art magazine The Jackdaw, described the works as "ghastly," while Robin Simon, editor of British Art Journal, said: "Thankfully, these sculptures are not going to be around for ever."

But Jay Jopling of the White Cube Gallery which exhibits Quinn, said: "I don't see how anyone could find this work sensationalist. It's a major work of art, drawing on tradition and context, very rich and layered."

And Bert Massie — chairman of the Disability Rights Commission — said: "Congratulations to Marc for realising that disabled bodies have a power and beauty rarely recognised in an age where youth and 'perfection' are idolised."

The committee — publicly funded to the tune of £80,000 a year — chose the winners from a shortlist of six, which included a Ford Fiesta covered in pigeon droppings and two wooden lifesize effigies of Tomahawk Cruise missiles.

Londoners had already given their own artistic judgement through an Evening Standard poll which suggested that around 70 per cent rejected all of the proposed works.

Tens of thousands more also messaged a plinth website with their suggestions about what statue or work should occupy the plinth.

The Greater London Authority admitted today that many of those voting on its website were against the idea of contemporary art in Trafalgar Square. Most would have preferred an iconic or historical figure to occupy the plinth, originally erected in 1841.

However, quite what it is Londoners said is today unclear — because the Mayor's committee refused to reveal which of the original six shortlisted works emerged as the favourite of the tens of thousands of people who expressed their opinion, either on the lavish Fourth Plinth website or at a National Gallery exhibition dedicated to displaying the choices.

Asked what the public's favourite was, Mr Nairne said: "All I'll say is that there were a lot of comments in different directions, positive and negative. What we were really interested in was getting a gauge."

He added: "At the end of the day it was an artistic judgement."

Editorial Comment: Page 11

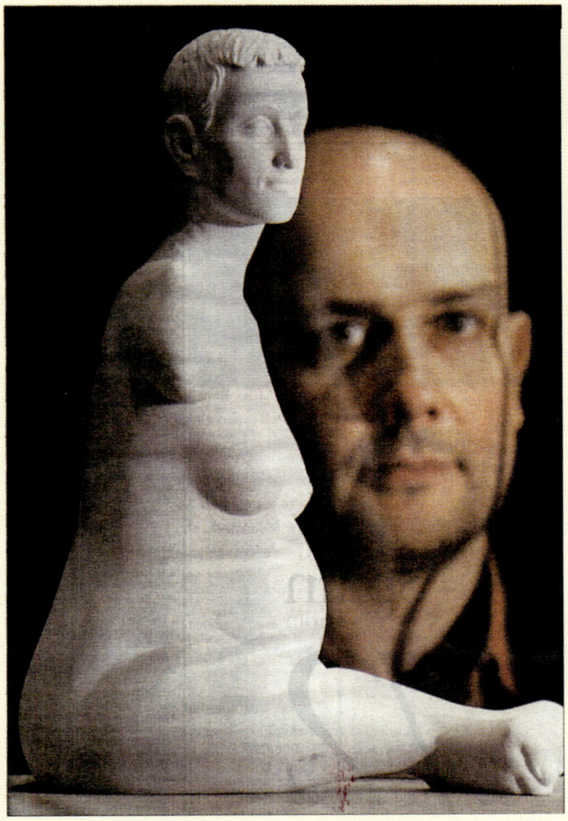

Choice: Marc Quinn with his statue Alison Lapper Pregnant, which will be displayed on the plinth for 18 months

'Nelson's Column is the epitome of a phallic male monument and I felt the square needed some femininity'
Marc Quinn, the artist

'It is a modern tribute to femininity, disability and motherhood'
Alison Lapper, the model

'I dislike the Quinn intensely and I can see no virtue in the Schütte'
Brian Sewell, Evening Standard art critic

'Both sculptures will be of compelling interest to Londoners and visitors'
Sandy Nairne, director of the National Portrait Gallery and chairman of the judges

'Whilst childbirth is a great thing to celebrate, I think we should have focused on individuals of great achievement the nation ought to commemorate'
Julie Kirkbride, Tory culture spokeswoman

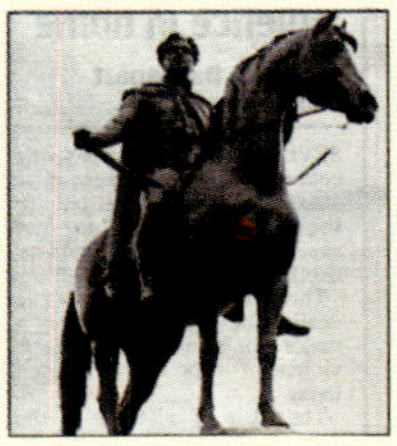

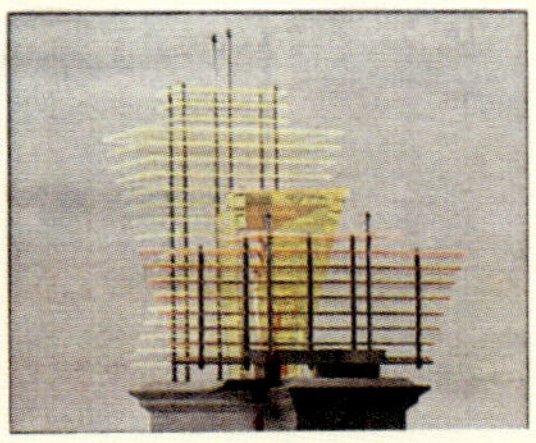

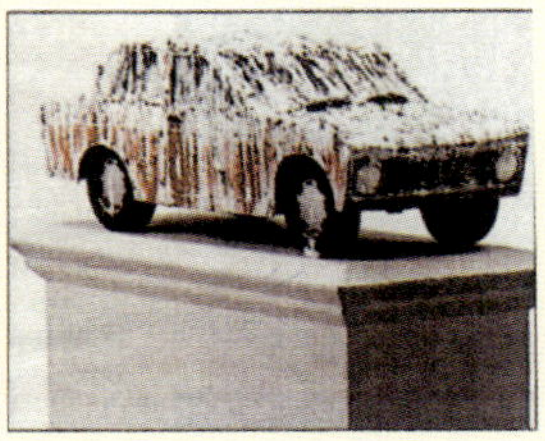

Is it art? Quinn's work will join the traditional statue of George IV, left, and will be replaced by Schütte's Hotel For The Birds. Right, one of the rejected works

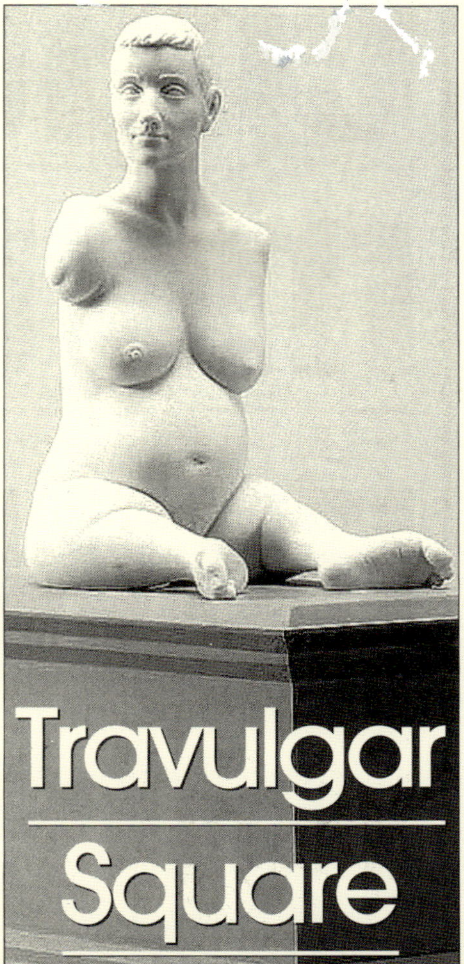

Travulgar Square

By STEVE KENNEDY

THE art world was in uproar last night after this statue of an armless pregnant woman was chosen for Trafalgar Square.

The politically-correct image of disabled mum-to-be Alison Lapper will stand for a year on the Square's empty fourth plinth, close to Nelson's Column.

The statue's creator, British artist Marc Quinn, 40, below, was "thrilled" when it was selected by a panel of experts.

But respected art critic Brian Sewell called it an "appalling", adding: "I would rather there was no statue at all."

Londoner Tim Harper, 31, said: "Trafalgar Square is about national pride and heroism. What does this say?"

The statue will be replaced in 2006 by a coloured perspex sculpture by German artist Thomas Schutte named Hotel For The Birds.

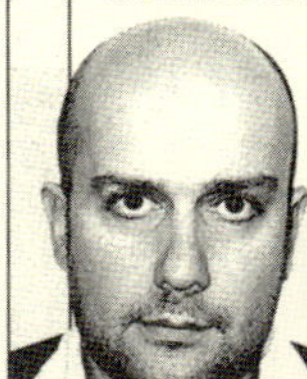

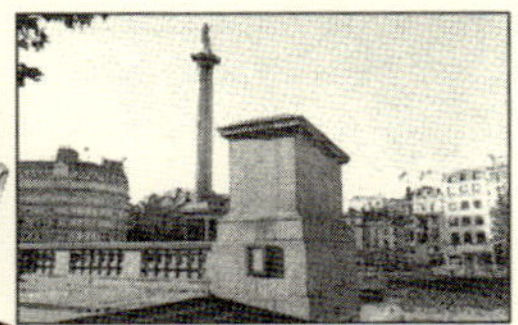

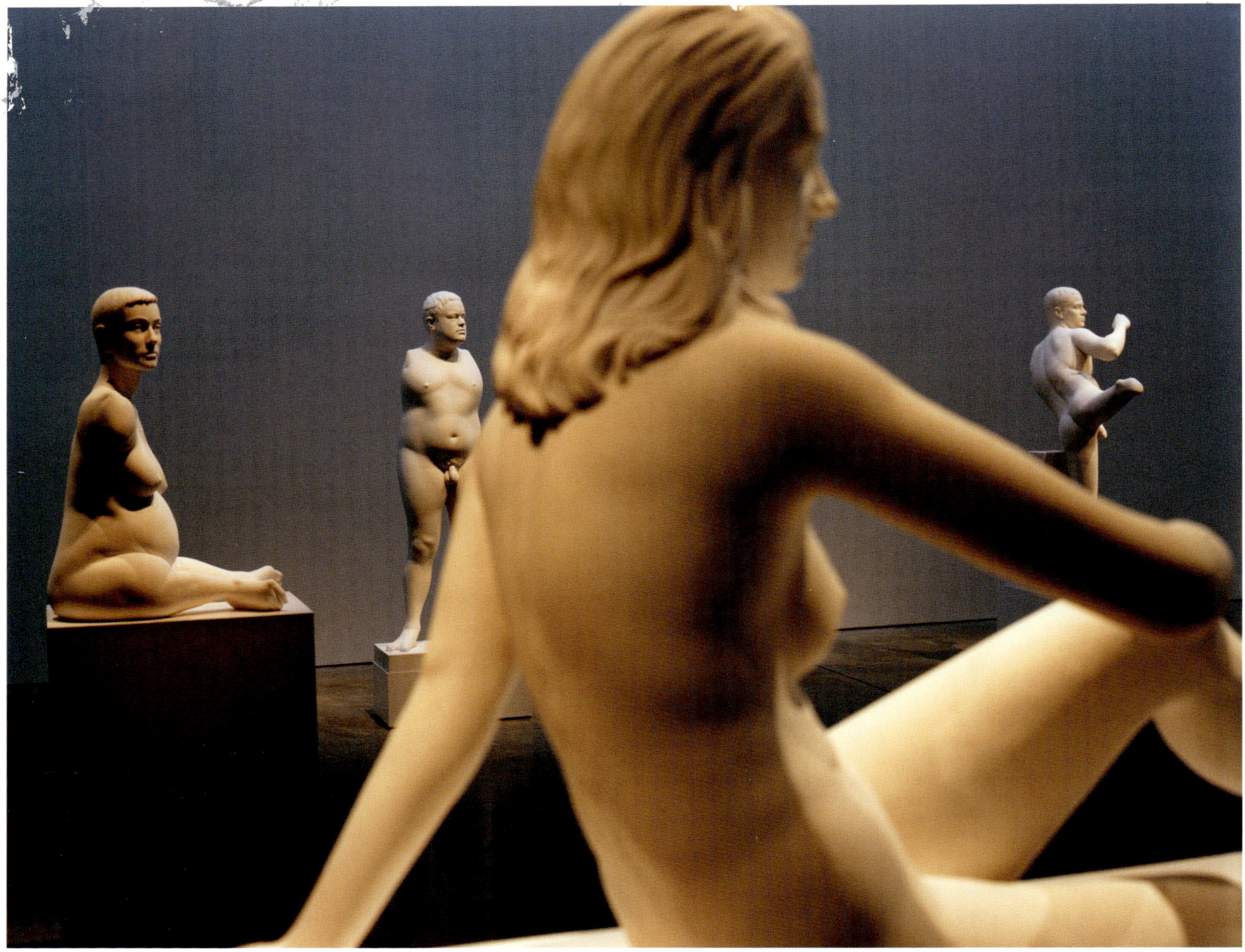

Installation view of *The Complete Marbles*,
Mary Boone Gallery, New York, January to March, 2004.

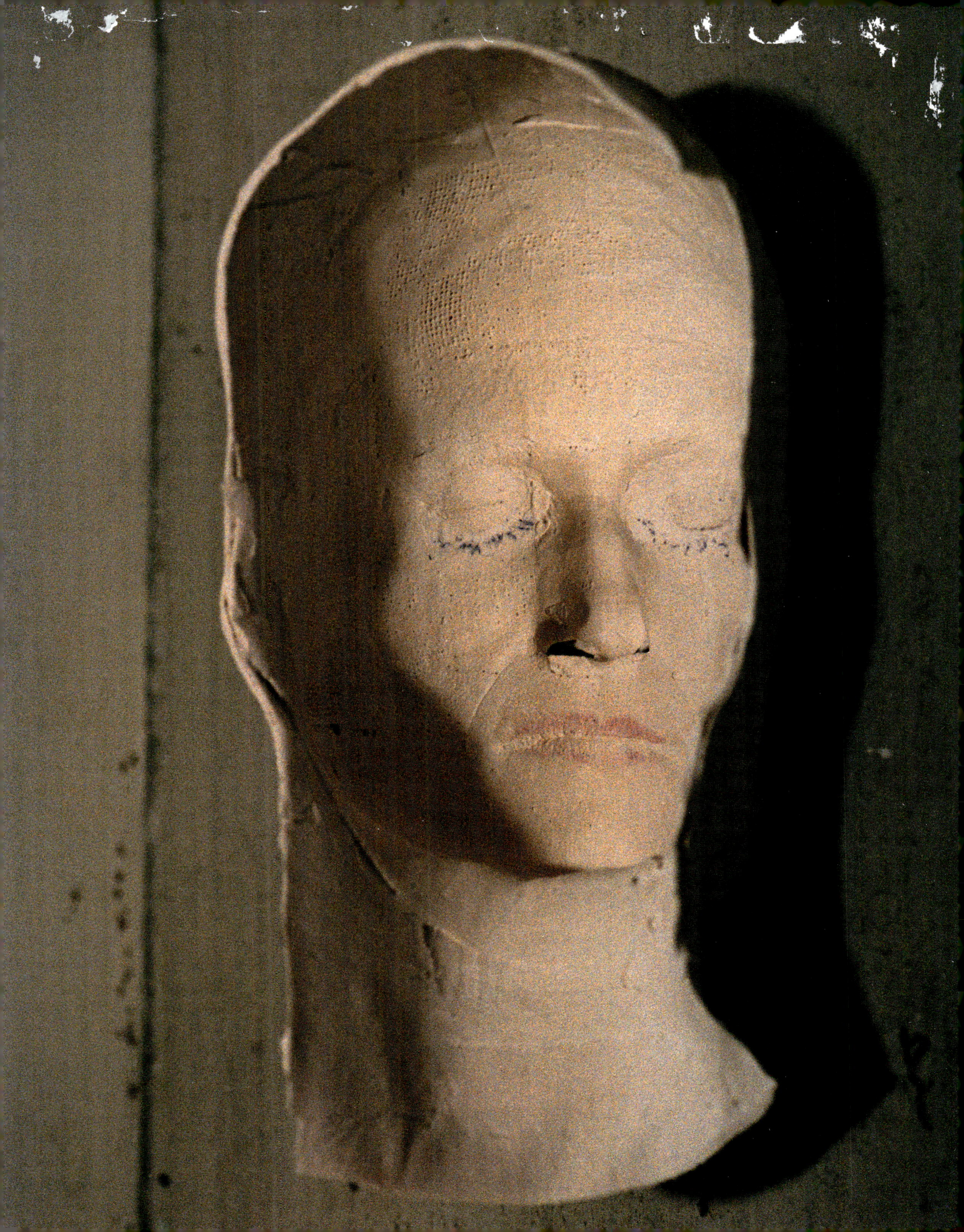

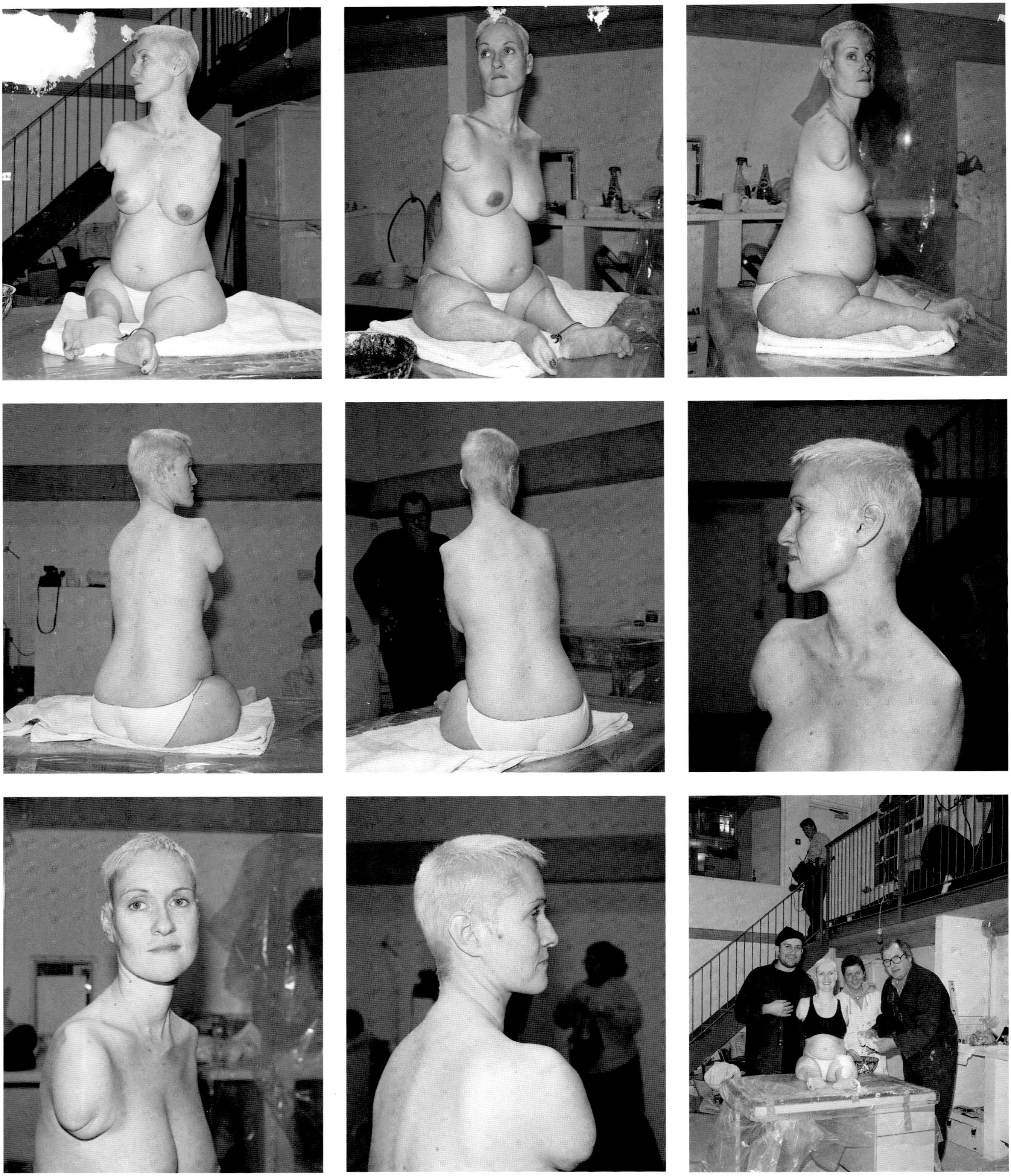

Alison Lapper during the making of the body cast at Marc Quinn's studio in 1999. The body cast was then used as the main reference point in the creation of both the marble life-size version of the portrait and the later colossal version. Noel Condon and Alexi Williams assisting.

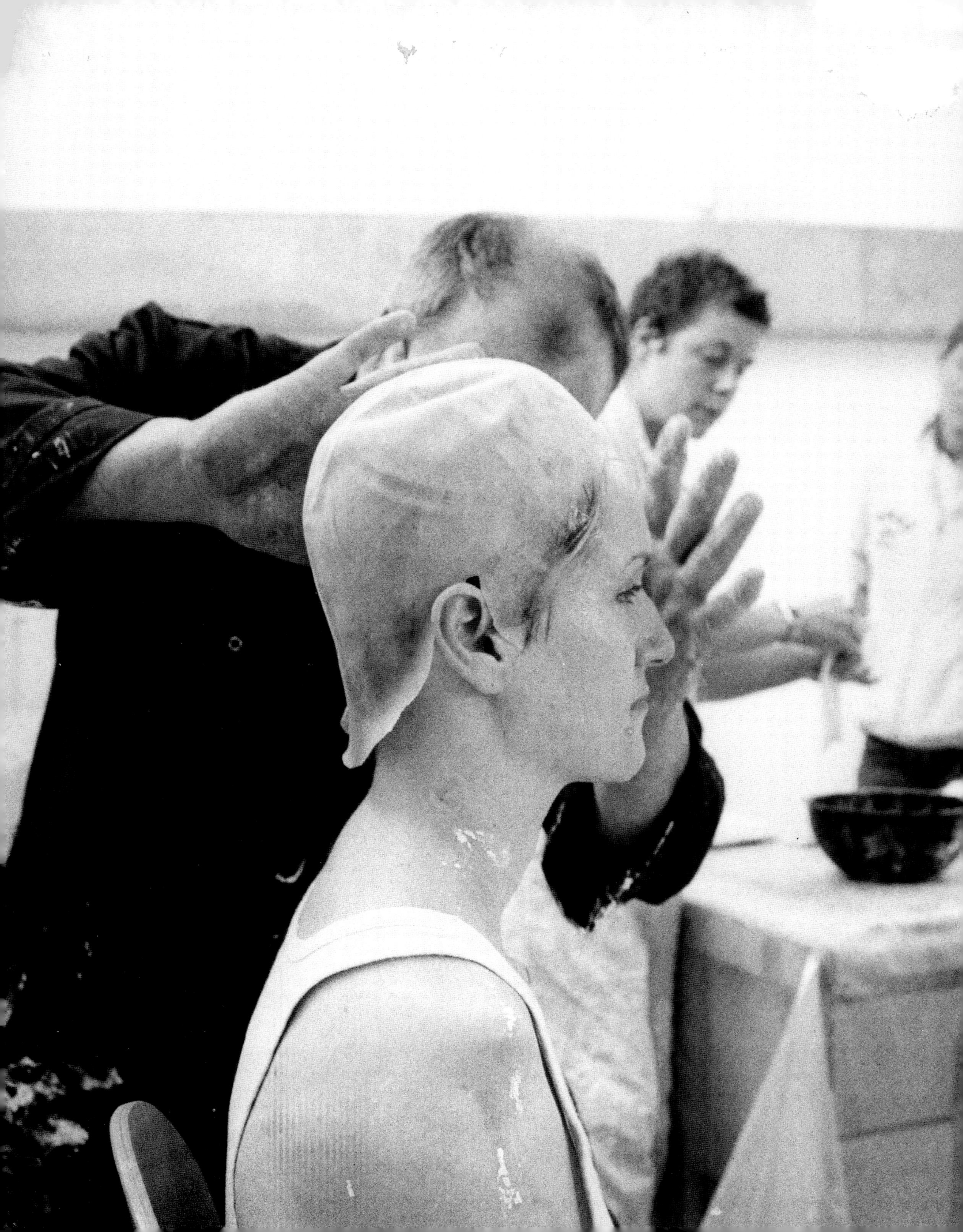

Nothing prepares you for the impact of Marc Quinn's extraordinary sculpture *Alison Lapper Pregnant*. The luminosity of the white marble flares like a torch against the gray backdrop of the National Gallery, and her head, huge and authoritative, determinedly turned away, holds its place with the spire of St Martins in the Field, the dome of the National Gallery, and Nelson's Column.

Sculpture is a public art and this sculpture, in a square that was once the heart of the British Empire, and is today the meeting place for all of London, has a constantly changing dialogue with the viewer.

Approaching the sculpture from behind across the newly pedestrianised expanse you are stunned by the epic size of the figure. Standing underneath her, all that is actually visible is a slice of her head with sternly cropped hair, and broad forehead of almost ancient nobility.

But then, back away, and the proud soldier disappears and you see the voluptuously pregnant torso of a naked, vulnerable woman.

A few steps later the absent arms are glimpsed – yet this is not a sculpture of a disabled person, but of a proud Helenic warrior. The very absence of limbs allows us to focus on the beauty of her head and torso.

The power of the sculpture lies in the fact that both these impressions – ancient and modern, mythical and realistic – continue after the initial surprise to exist in tandem, resulting in a wonderful series of paradoxes. The dialogue of opposites also exists, crucially, between the sculpture and the square. The other figures are statesmen, generals, clothed in the regalia of their public personae and status: this is the only female, the only nude, the only figure left unadorned.

Quite simply, the beauty of this work of art exists on its own terms, and apart from the numberless moral conclusions which can be drawn from it. Its very limbless simplicity, concentrating the energy into the centre of the figure, reduces the form to its essence; the play of light and shadow on this mass, with its luminous weight, its quiet strength, makes the ordinary subject extraordinary.

It is my belief that this great public sculpture should stand permanently in a major public space. It should stay in Trafalgar Square.

Richard Rogers

Mary Kenny The beautiful sculpture Alison Lapper Pregnant is a total vindication for the pro-life campaigners of the 60s

Living proof

Some time in the spring of 2005, a beautiful sculpture of a disabled, naked, pregnant woman, will be placed on the empty fourth plinth in Trafalgar Square. Marc Quinn's marble work, Alison Lapper Pregnant, has already created a storm of controversy. Some critics regard it as an example of political correctness taken to extremes, and have pointed to the predominantly leftwing flavour of the Fourth Plinth Commissioning Group.

Yet, paradoxically, the elevation of Alison Lapper to a 15ft statue could be described as a triumph for the pro-life lobby which, 38 years ago, when Alison Lapper was born without arms and with flapper-like legs, was the only group which thought she was entitled to exist. The "leftwing" activists at the time were, with the thalidomide scandal raging, campaigning for people like Alison (whose condition results from a congenital disorder called phocomelia) to be terminated in the womb. Indeed, the majority of the public, back in the mid-60s, felt that the thalidomide drug had inflicted such gross deformities that abortion should be legalised particularly for this purpose.

The thalidomide scandal, moreover, proved to be exactly what the Abortion Law Reform Association (the lobby seeking to legalise abortion) needed to clinch its cause. "The drug thalidomide was the motor that reinvigorated the Abortion Law Reform Association and paved the way for reform," wrote Keith Hindell and Madeleine Simms in Abortion Law Reformed, their comprehensive 1971 account of the change in the law. Up until the thalidomide scandal, the abortion lobby had found it difficult to break through the ingrained public and parliamentary opposition. Alra found its way blocked by respectable opinion — which feared that easy abortion would cause a drop in moral standards — by the pro-life movements, and the influence of the Catholic church.

It had campaigned for legalisation so as to halt the scandal of back-street abortions — which were horribly high in the desperate 30s, when more than 400 women a year died. But by the 60s, deaths from illegal abortions had fallen virtually to zero because of modern antibiotics and because termination was being practiced de facto in hospital conditions (the pre-1967 law allowed for a certain amount of flexible interpretation). Of course, there was a heavy element of hypocrisy, and secrecy, but the British public, or its parliament, were not about to vote merely to remove hypocrisy and secrecy. There was a prevailing view that there should be deterrents to easy abortion.

The notion of "choice" was not an issue in the 60s. This arose after the American debates of the 70s, when "a woman's right to choose" was so successfully marketed as a slogan. Before that, campaigners were anxious to put over serious concerns for hard cases: the over-burdened mother of six or the rape victim. So when the thalidomide scandal struck in the early 60s, it was the secular version of an answer to prayer.

From that moment onwards, the reformers sensed that theirs was no longer a minority movement but had mass support. The case of Sherri Finkbine of Phoenix, Arizona, made particular news in the summer of 1962: she had taken thalidomide early in her pregnancy, and had to fly to Sweden for a termination. Vatican Radio condemned this, but public opinion supported Mrs Finkbine. The cartoonist Trog drew a brilliant cartoon in Private Eye in which a pompous, pinstriped doctor looks down his nose at a distressed young woman: "I'm sorry," he says, "but the ethical position is quite clear — thalidomide was a legal prescription, but what you suggest is an illegal operation."

> The thalidomide scandal was the secular version of an answer to a prayer

And so it turned out, just as Hindell and Simms wrote: thalidomide made abortion acceptable. A Daily Mail/NOP opinion poll found that 80% of the public now supported a change in the law for such dreadful deformities. Only the pro-life movements and the Catholic church stubbornly maintained that a thalidomide baby — or any disabled child — still had the right to life, though Hindell and Simms were pleased to note that "under the impact of the harsh reality of this tragedy [of thalidomide], the authority of Catholic dogma silently disintegrated".

Scroll forward some 40 years: and the principle that a child with severe disabilities indeed has the right to live is cast in stone by Alison Lapper Pregnant. The admirable Lapper certainly did have a hard time as a baby. Her birth mother was told that Alison was too ugly to live, and doctors considered her "a cabbage". She was brought up in foster care, but overcame her many difficulties and disadvantages to gain a first in fine art at Brighton University, and to become a delighted mother herself.

Some traditionalists wanted a statue of Elizabeth, the late Queen Mum, on the spare plinth. But as Alison herself remarked lightly, there are enough statues of dead characters there already: "At least I'm alive, and people should celebrate that." And isn't Alison's living, and fertile, status a celebration of human life — and even for the forces of pro-life?

Mary Kenny is a freelance author and journalist. She is the author of Abortion: The Whole Story mary@mary-kenny.com

COMMENT & ANALYSIS

JANET STREET-PORTER » EDITOR-AT-LARGE

Like it or not, we get the art we deserve

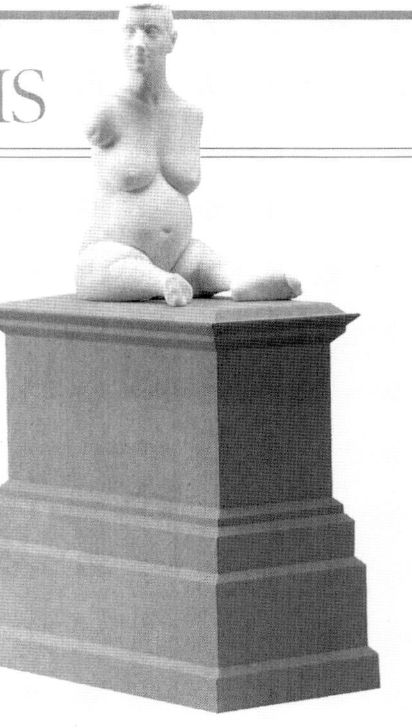

'Alison Lapper pregnant', the sculpture by Marc Quinn that has been chosen for the fourth plinth in Trafalgar Square
PA

I'll say one thing, those BritArt people have certainly cornered the business of enraging Middle England, haven't they? Charles Saatchi's latest exhibition (wittily entitled *New Blood*) doesn't open until Wednesday and already a row has started over the work of stripper-turned-painter Stella Vine. Vine's portraits of a miserable Princess of

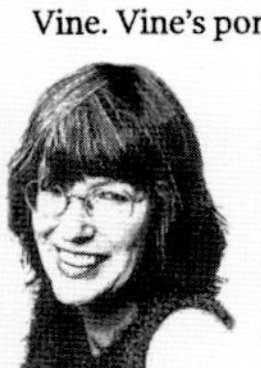

of Wales and the dead heroin addict Rachel Whitear have caused major "offence", according to the press, shades of the Myra Hindley portrait by Marcus Harvey in the *Sensation* exhibition at the Royal Academy a few years ago.

Although Vine has pictured Rachel as a charming schoolgirl her parents are said to be mortified that an artist has dared to add to the controversy surrounding the tragic circumstances of their daughter's demise. Her body is now being exhumed as the police continue to examine the exact cause of her death which must be distressing for her family, but I cannot for the life of me see why Vine's artistic endeavours should be so castigated. When Rachel's parents allowed shocking pictures of her dead body to be used in an anti-drug campaign, I am afraid they placed their family in the public domain. Stella Vine's work may not be to your taste, but frankly, one young woman producing an iconic image of another seems pretty OK to me.

Let's also consider the reception that Marc Quinn has faced since his proposed larger-than-life sculpture of Alison Lapper, a victim of the congenital disorder phocomelia, was chosen to adorn the empty plinth in Trafalgar Square. Miss Lapper will be shown naked and heavily pregnant. She has no arms and extremely shortened legs. I wasn't too pleased when Ken Livingstone announced the competition for this piece of public art, as it seemed a case of political opportunism on his part. And using £160,000 of public money to fund six maquettes and the dreaded consultation process seemed shameful when the artists could have donated models for free for the publicity.

But the committee, chaired by Sandy Nairne, director of the National Portrait Gallery, has come up with a winner that we can be proud of. I'm not so keen on the lego-like *Hotel for the Birds* by German artist Thomas Schutte which will follow Quinn's sculpture, but there we are. Now sponsorship of £300,000 is being sought to fund the two pieces, which is good news. But what I admire about Marc Quinn's work is that he, like Stella Vine, has managed to touch on a raw nerve with his depiction of 21st-century femininity. Roy Hattersley was quick off the draw, predictably enough in the *Daily Mail*. Mr Hattersley thinks that Trafalgar Square should be used to celebrate British greatness, and that the statue of Nelson, who lost an eye and an arm, already celebrates a triumph over disability. Alice Thomson in the *Telegraph* went nuts because Quinn had the temerity to suggest that perhaps Nelson's column was a phallic symbol, and it's about time we had an antidote. Alice feels that Alison is rendered in a "chillingly impersonal way" and that her own achievements as an artist don't get a look-in, and the result is "shocking, bad art". Doesn't the girl have any sense of irony?

Alison herself has a different perspective. She says "disabled artists don't get exhibitions. But now I'm up there. You can't avoid me any more." Most of the modern art on public display in London has been funded by private developers, in places such as Broadgate and Canary Wharf. Walking around the giant sculpture by Fernando Botero at the back of Liverpool Street Station is a delightful experience of which we need more. Public art doesn't have to honour anyone. Let's just celebrate the fact that Britain has produced contemporary artists and architects of world rank, and perhaps consider that very few of our politicians would merit being turned into a bird bath, let alone a monumental likeness in one of the great piazzas of Europe. Each decade gets the art it deserves, and with Stella Vine and Marc Quinn, we are making history.

Don't do it, Esther

Is there a cut-off point at which you turn down a job because it's simply too degrading? I ask because the prospect of watching – in my living room – Esther Rantzen find a new husband on BBC2 is one bit of reality TV I will be only too pleased to avoid. Esther is older than me, and obviously a great deal more thick-skinned. She must be suffering from severe fame withdrawal to contemplate participating in such a demeaning process, as one of the "contestants", if that's the right word, on a new series of *Would Like to Meet*. As BBC2 decides to celebrate the older generation, Esther was straight off the starting blocks, offering to take advice on what to wear and how to flirt. Get a life! I may have been unsuccessfully married four times, but at least I made all my choices of my own free will, not urged on by cameramen, pushy producers or channel controllers anxious to employ ever more desperate stunts to attract ratings. Now a lecturer at Keele University has identified 27 types of male, which could make Esther's selection process a lot easier. Sadly, this academic didn't come up with the one category I seem to specialise in – Unsuitable. I feel a "Dear Esther, please get a grip" letter coming on.

Too modern for me

The Coliseum, home of the English National Opera, has just reopened after a huge refurbishment programme. This wonderful building looks thoroughly revitalised, with a new space in the fabulous tower, loads more ladies' toilets and better places to sit, eat and drink while you have a culturally enriching night out. Sadly, Phyllida Lloyd's new production of Wagner's *Rhinegold*, in modern dress just wasn't magical enough for their first endeavour. The most successful films in the world in recent years have been the *Lord of the Rings* trilogy – fairy stories involving complicated mythology set in complicated worlds with dark secrets and strange language.

So what is to be gained by setting Wagner's tale in something that looks like a cheap flat in Fulham? The bathroom fittings were so ghastly (the wash basin didn't match the loo or the bath) I could barely concentrate. The evening kicked off with three Rhine maidens clad in blue, sequinned minis pole-dancing. One could dance and sing; another could sing and not dance; and one was just embarrassed by the whole idea. I noted that Spearmint Rhino was credited in the programme and I would love to have been a fly on the wall during the "research" sessions at one of their salubrious establishments.

In Lloyd's production, Alberich, in a gangster's bright red suit, is envisaged as a feeble version of Steven Berkoff. Asking singers to sing and act is one thing. Asking sopranos to sing and lap-dance demeans both skills. Wagner's music is haunting, revolutionary and remarkably accessible. Placing his grand concept in the present adds nothing, and ends up being faintly patronising. It reduces a masterpiece to a bit of second-rate musical theatre. And don't let's even discuss the appalling libretto in English. It was about as magical as reading the instructions that came with my new steam iron.

Charles Darwent, ABC, page 16

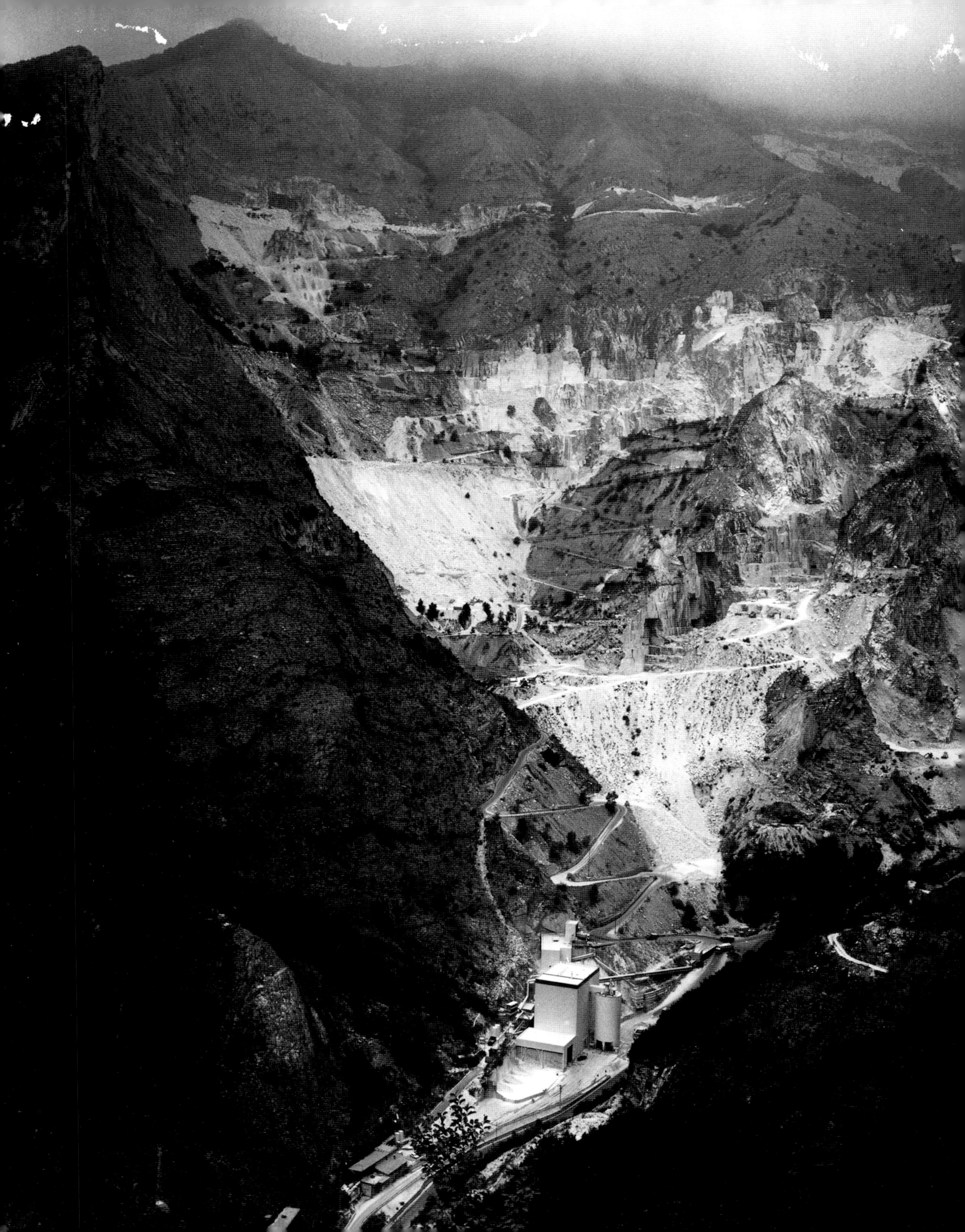

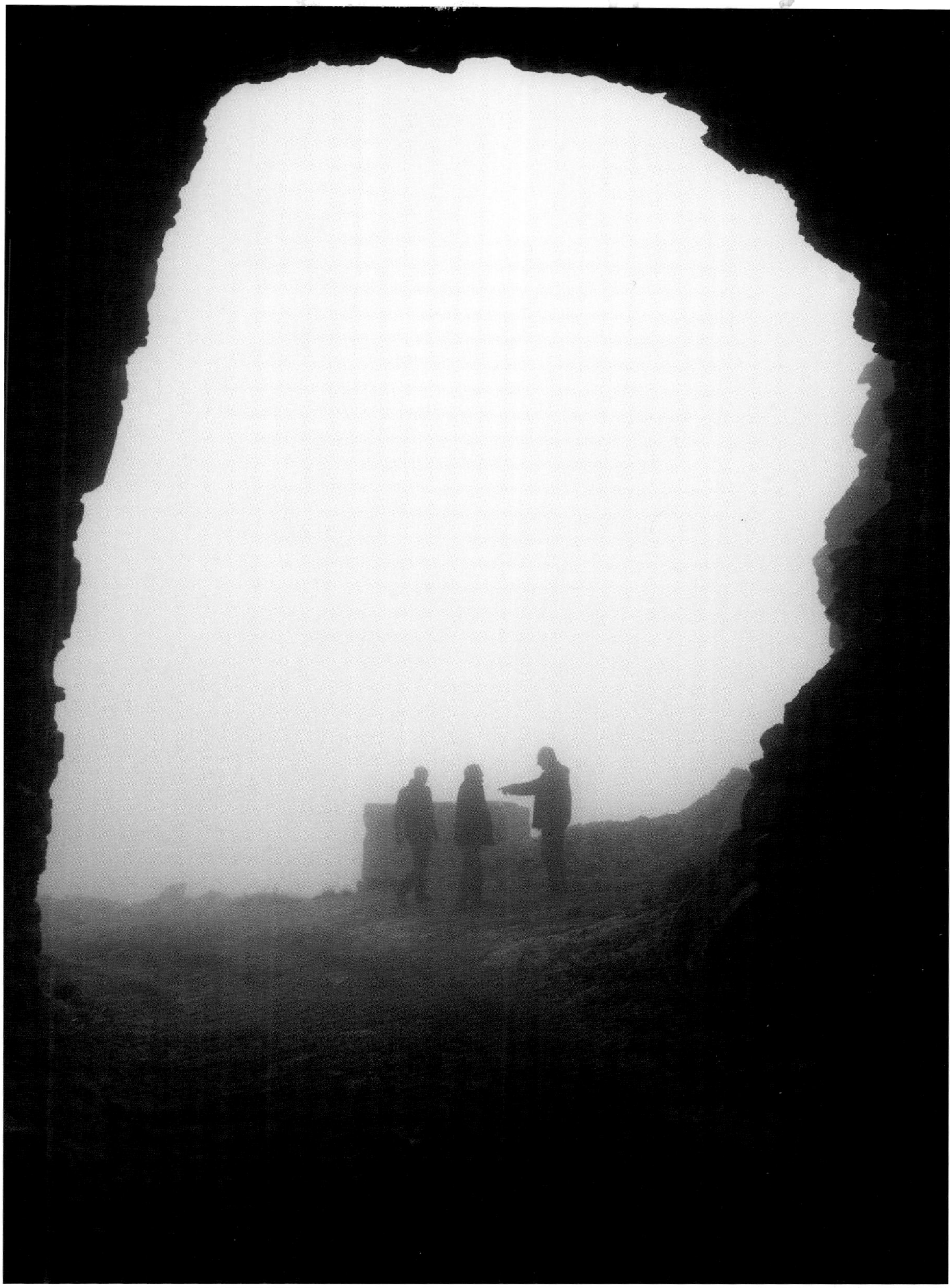

Left: Mountain, Carrara, Italy 1999.
Above: October 2004. Entrance to Piastreta quarry, Massa, source of the marble for the sculpture on the day the block is to be cut. Due to the altitude clouds shroud the mountain. In silhouette quarry owner Umberto Ronchieri and stone yard owner Franco Cervietti confer with a quarry worker.
Overpage: Marc Quinn in the interior of the mountain.

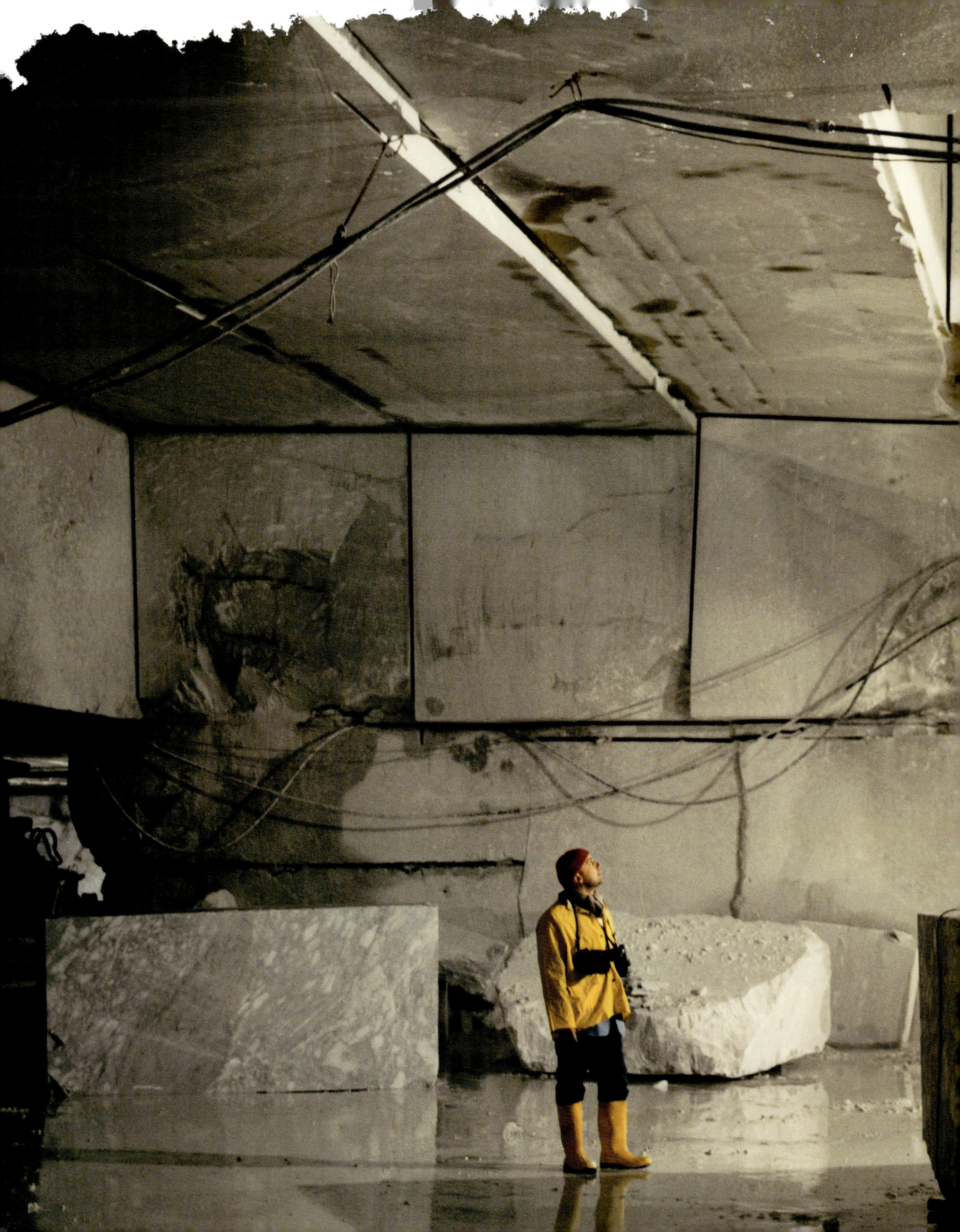

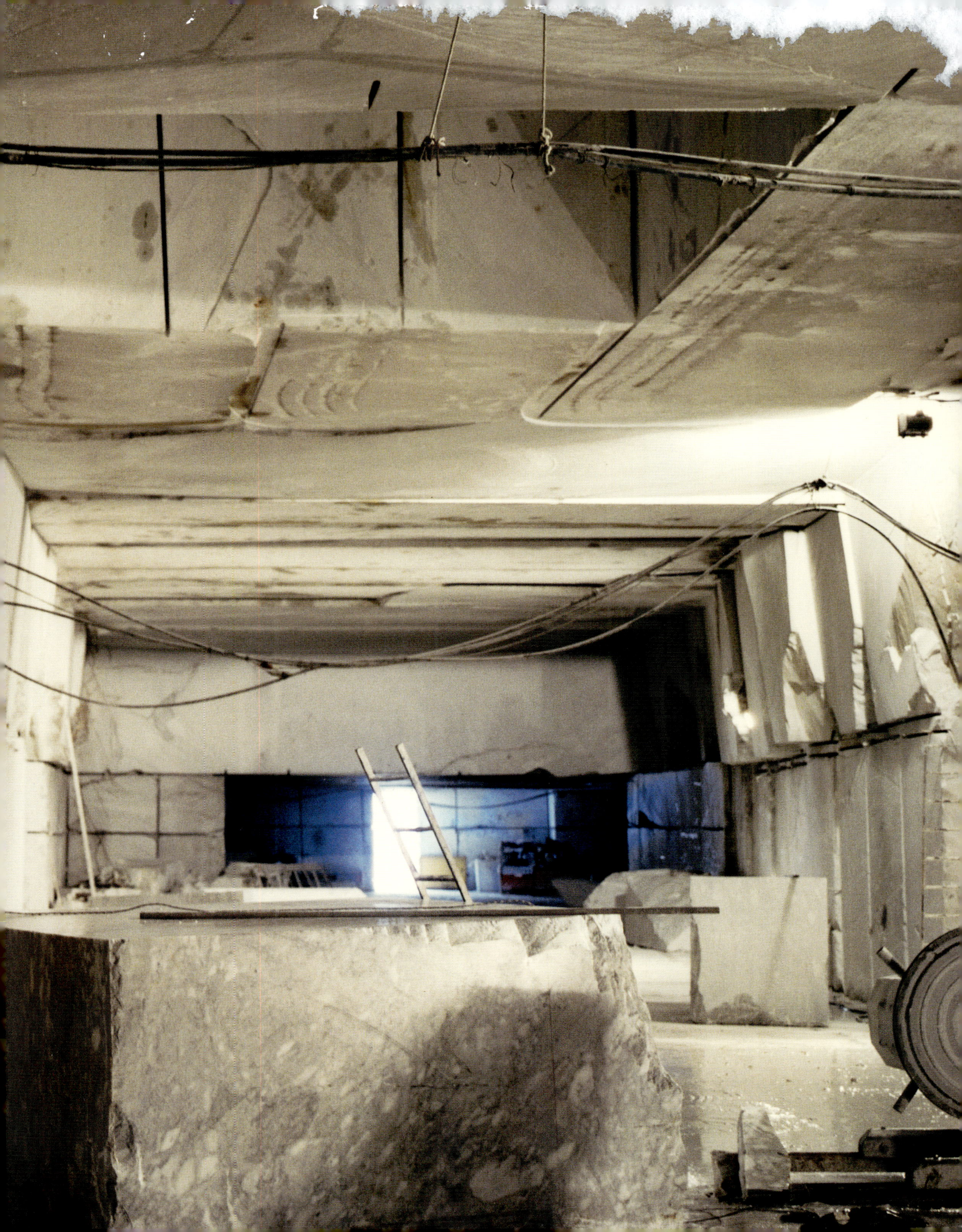

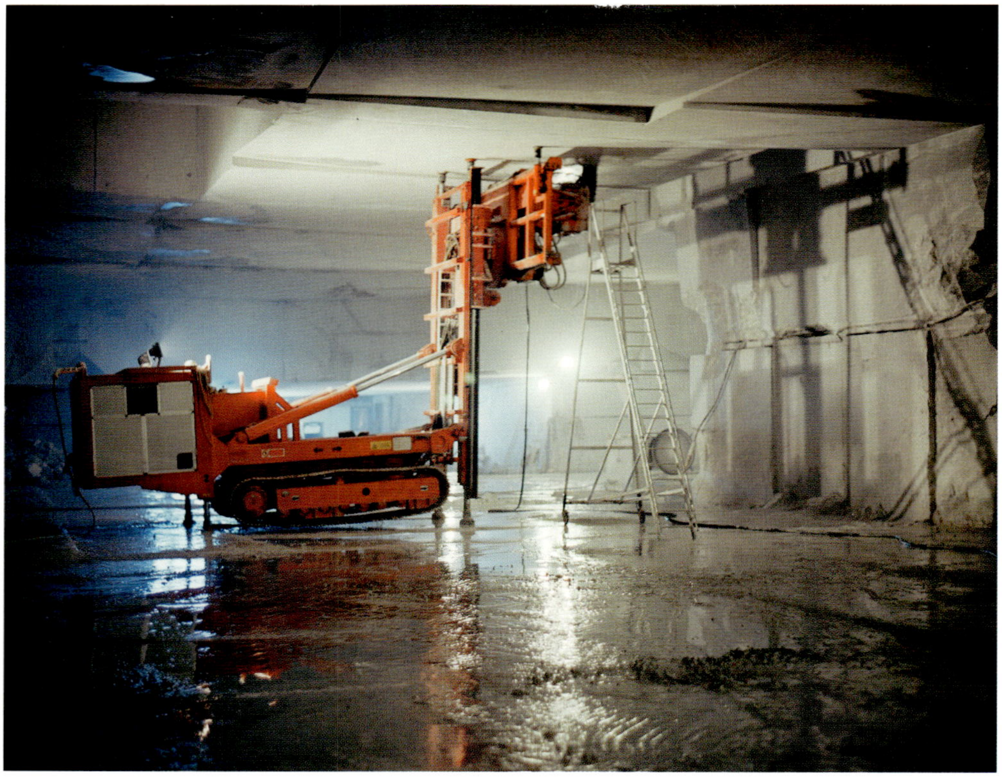

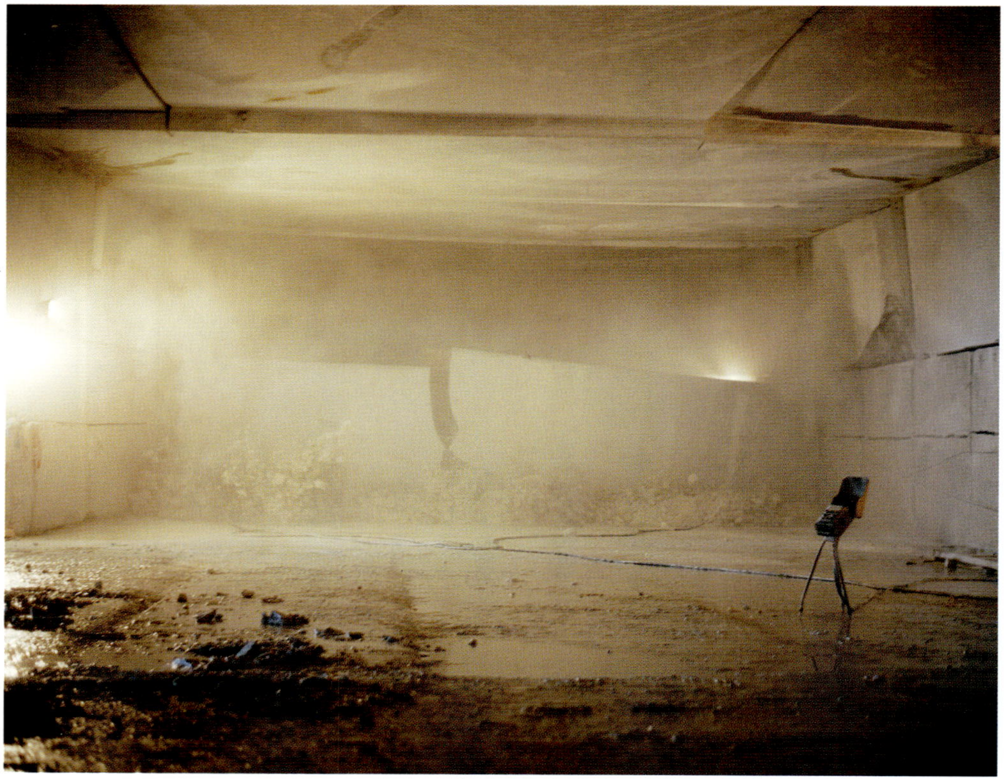

The block of *Bianco P* marble which is to form the sculpture is cast from the ceiling of the gallery within the mountain. The block is left to crash to the floor to test it for faults or cracks.

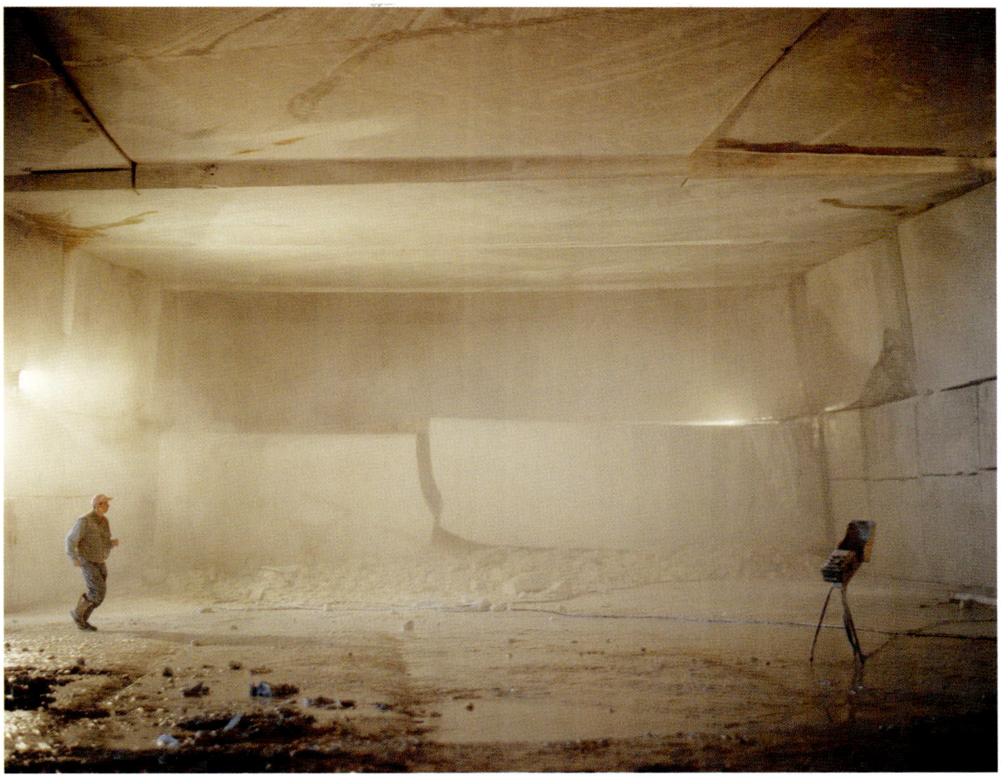

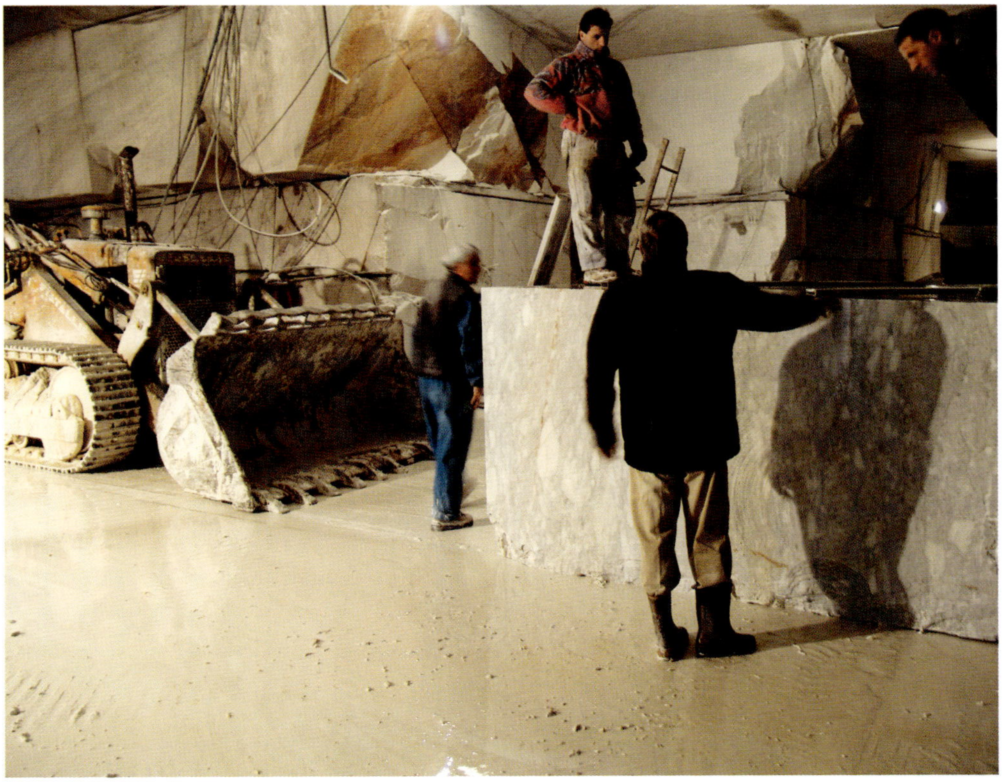

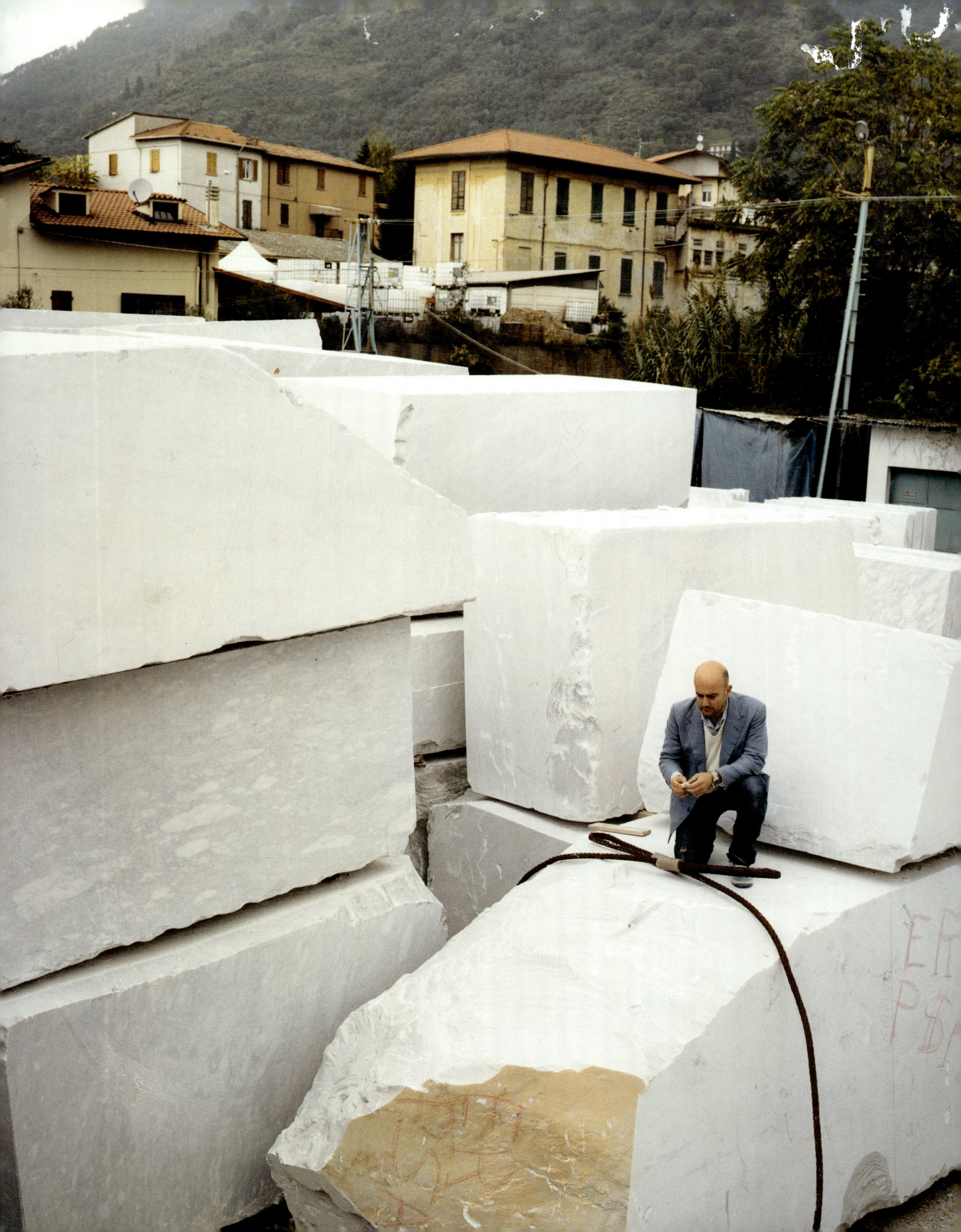

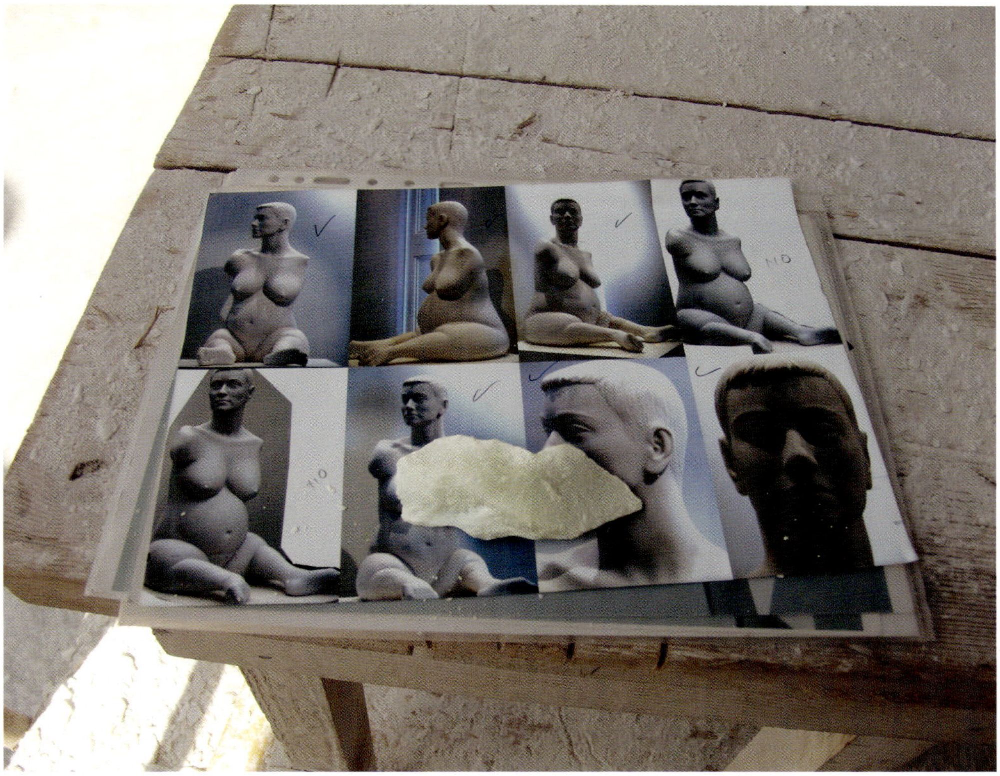

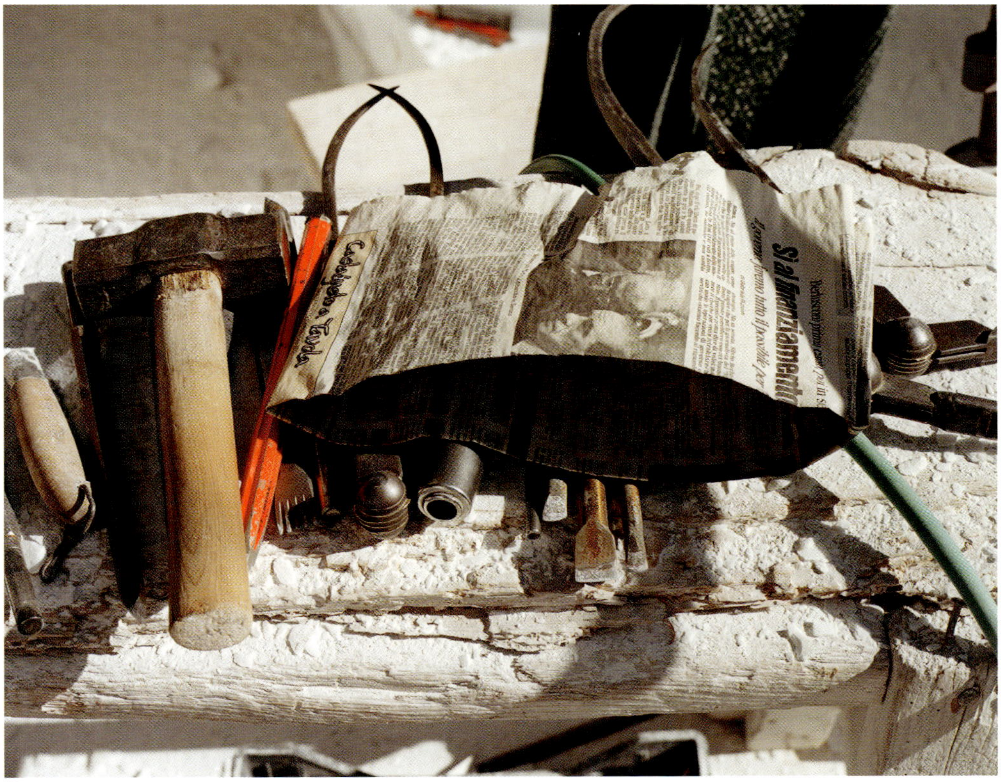

Opposite: Artist on the block selected for the work in Rocnchieri stone yard, Massa.
Above: At Cervietti *Laboratory* in Pietrasanta. Using tools and techniques that have hardly changed for centuries the statue is carved by hand with reference to photographs of the original life-size portrait.

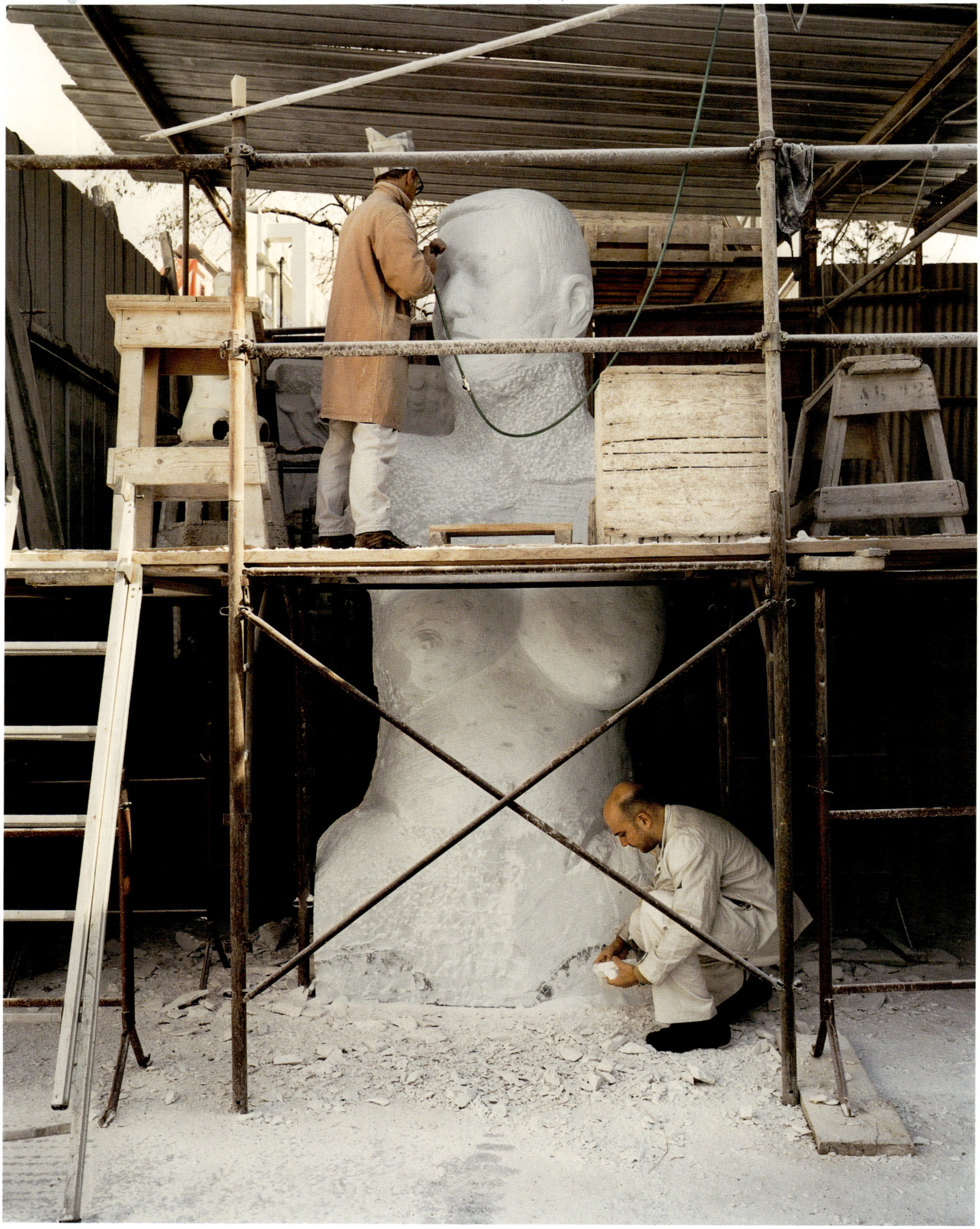

Italo Lenzoni works on the face of the sculpture
at Cervietti *Laboratory* in Pietrasanta, Italy.
He is using a compressed air-driven chisel.

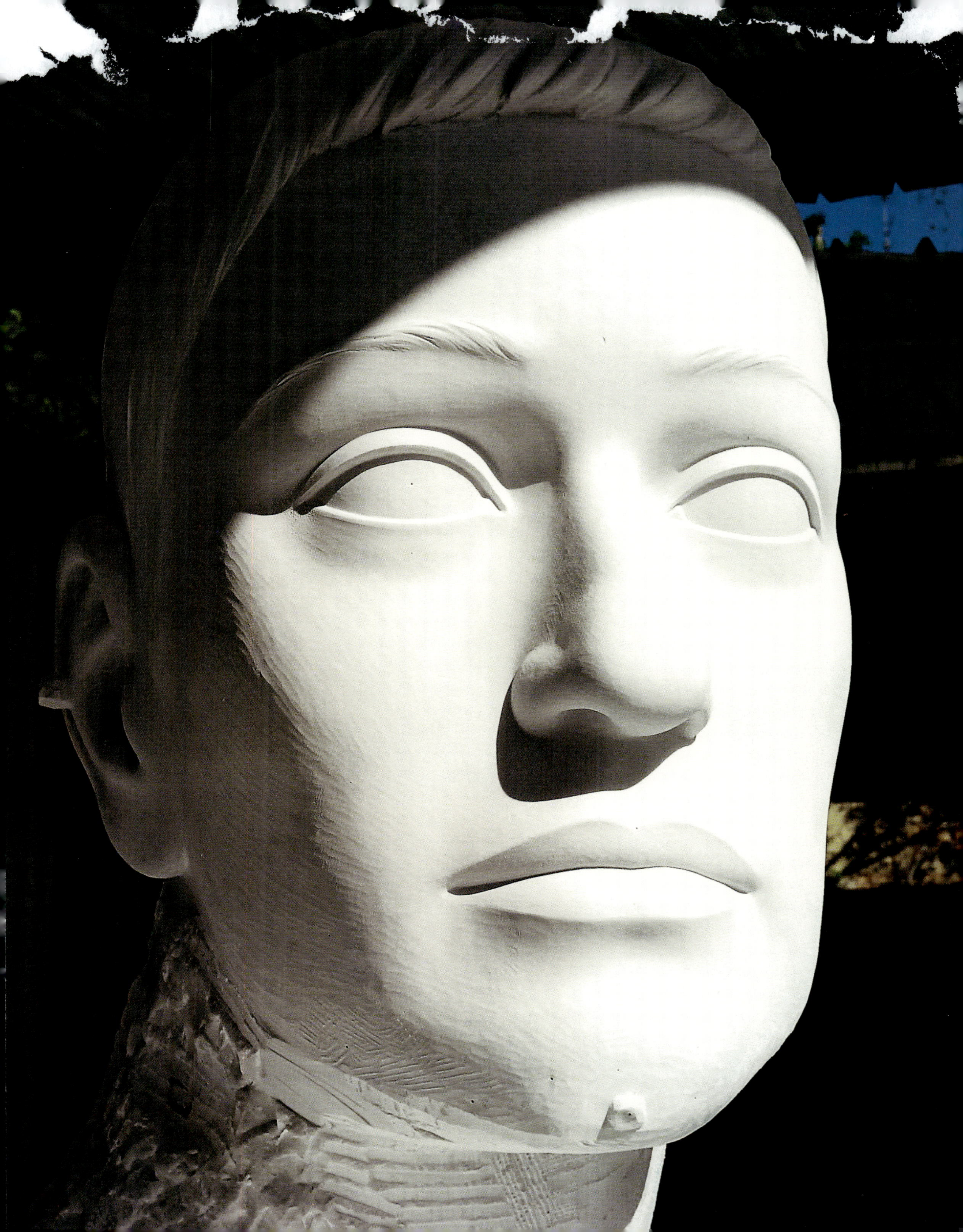

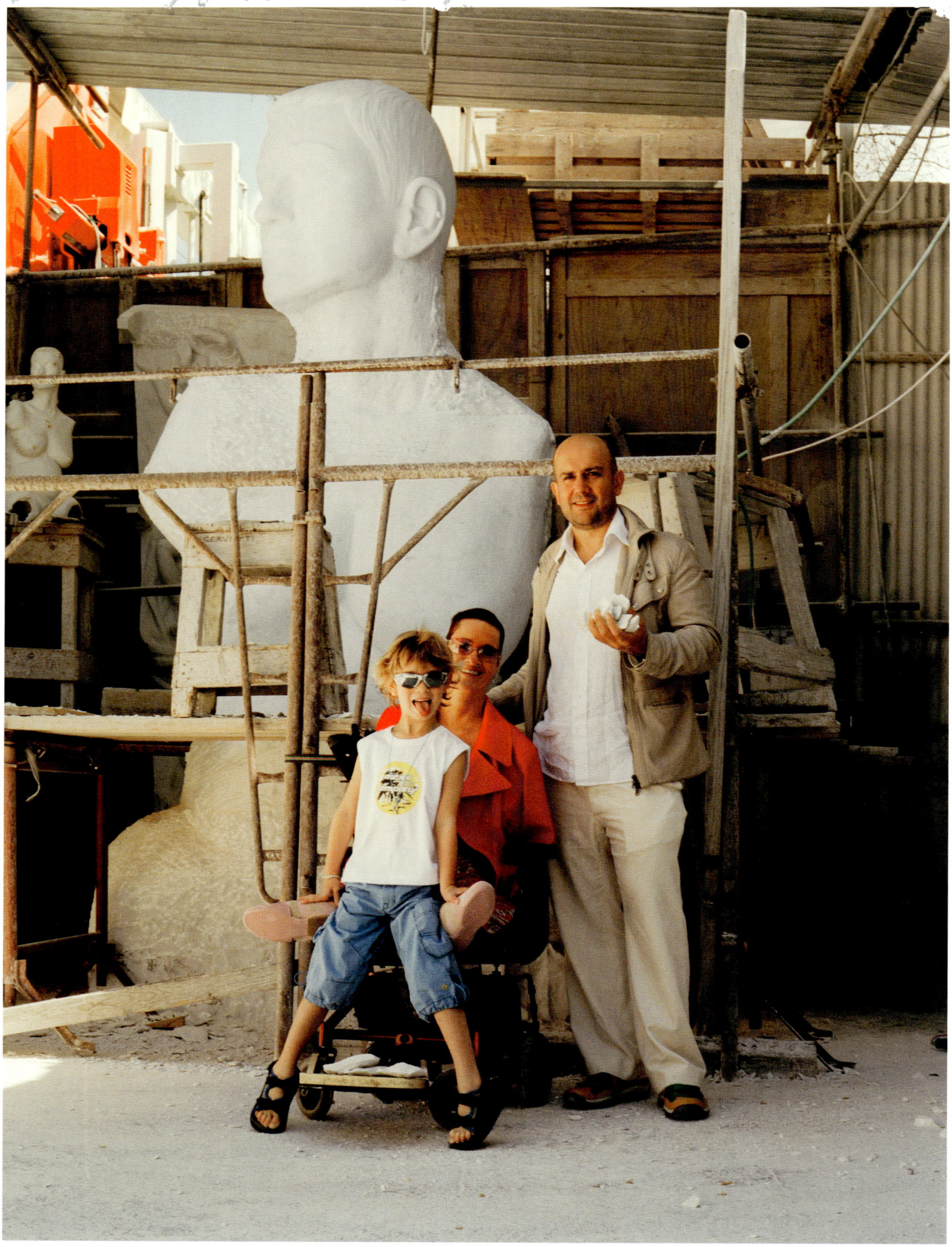

Above: Alison Lapper and her son Parys visit Cervetti stone yard to see work in progress. Spring 2005.
Opposite: The finished sculpture in August 2005, with the original life cast maquette on the left.

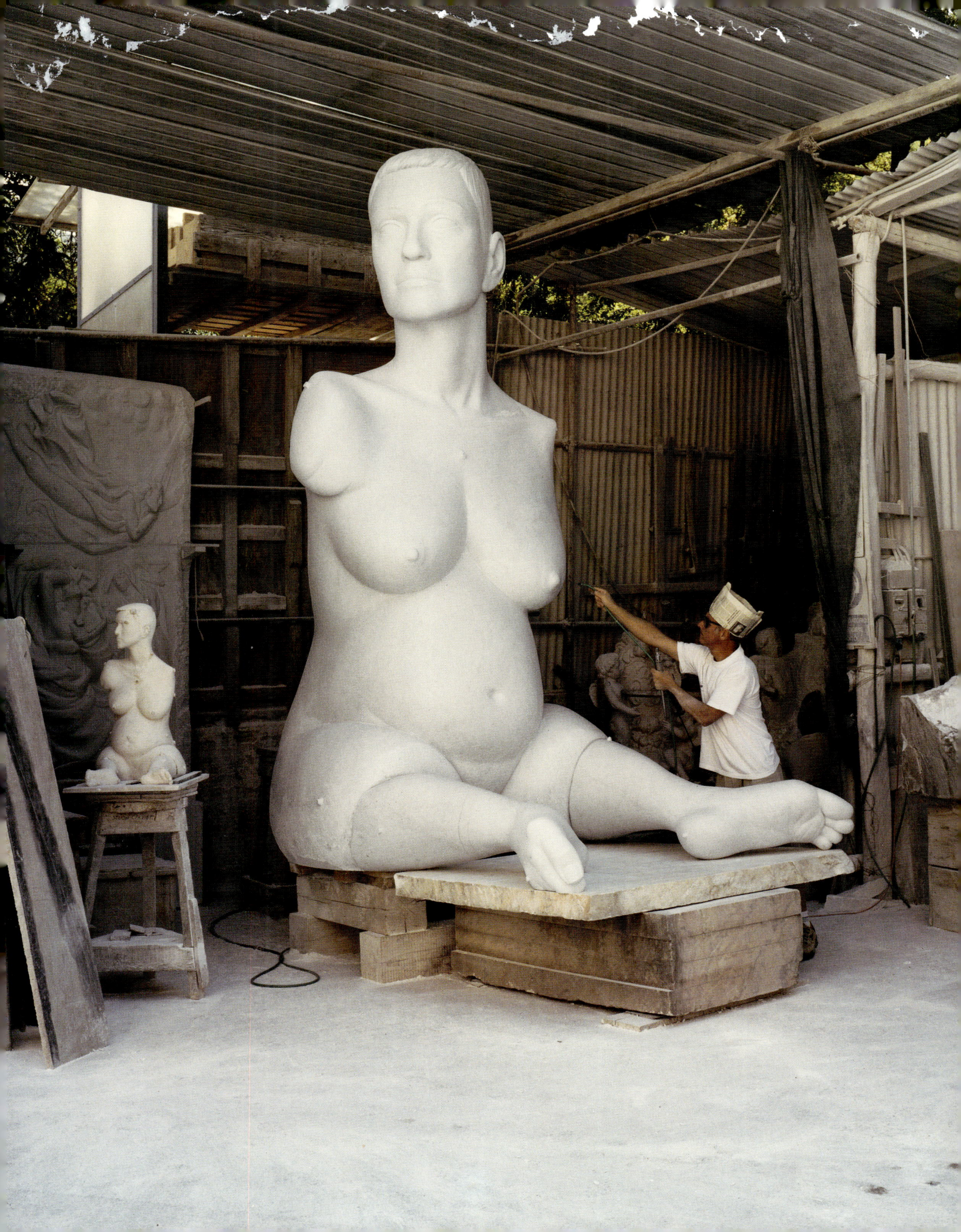

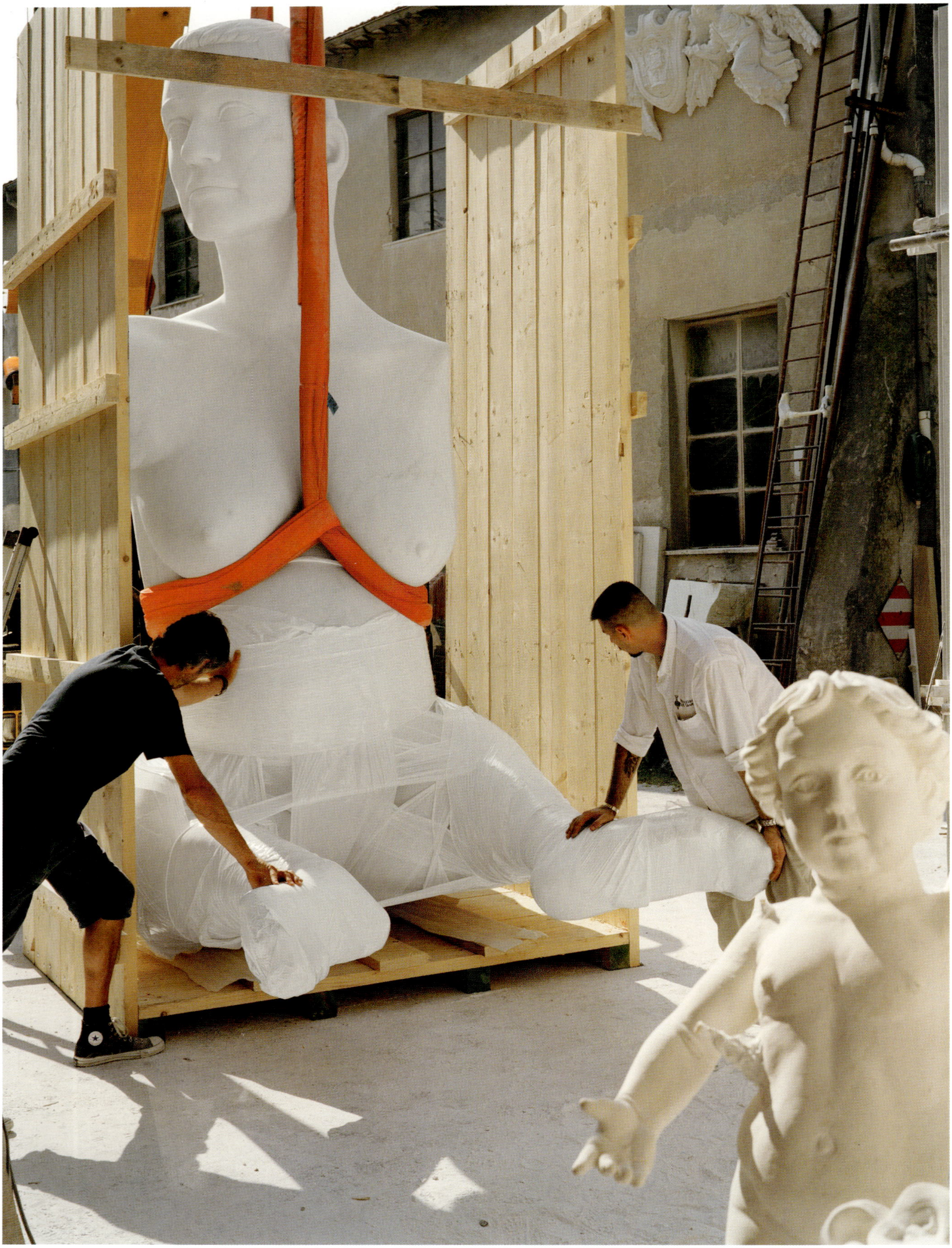

Above: September 2005. The completed sculpture is carefully packed for transport by road and channel tunnel to London.
Opposite: September 2005. Upon arrival in Trafalgar Square a crane hoists the sculpture onto the Fourth Plinth.

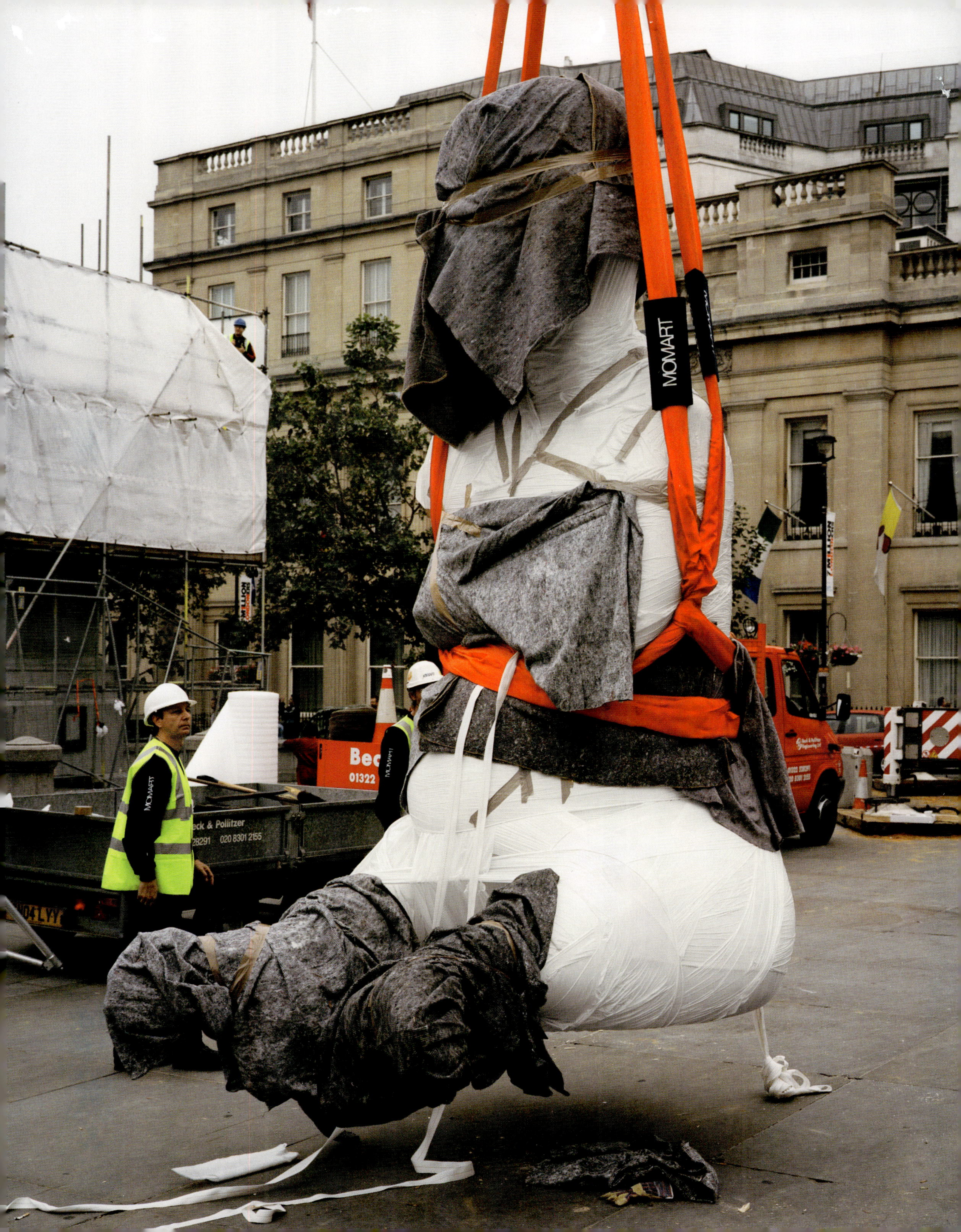
MOMART

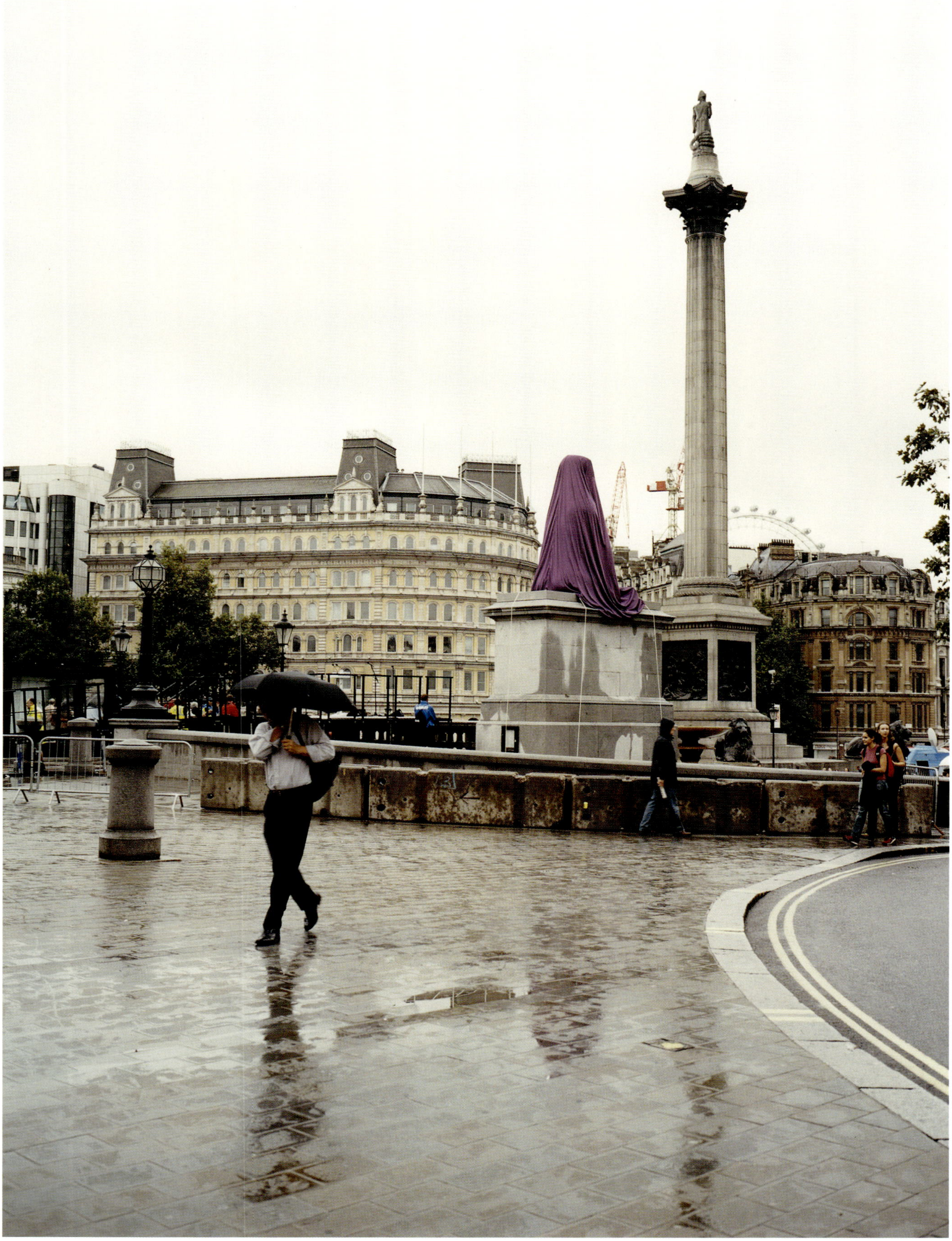

Sculpture prior to unveiling on 15 September, 2005.

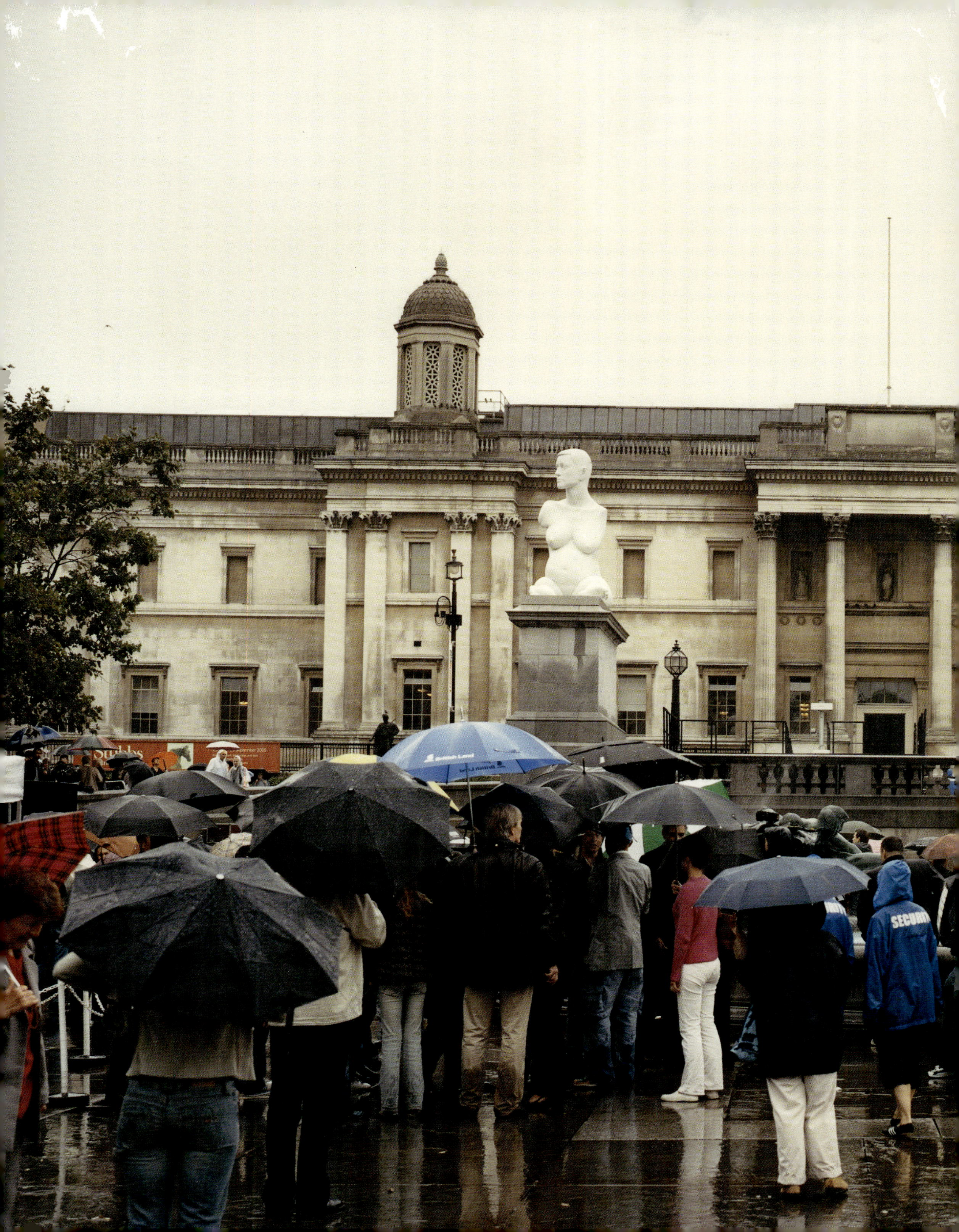
British Land

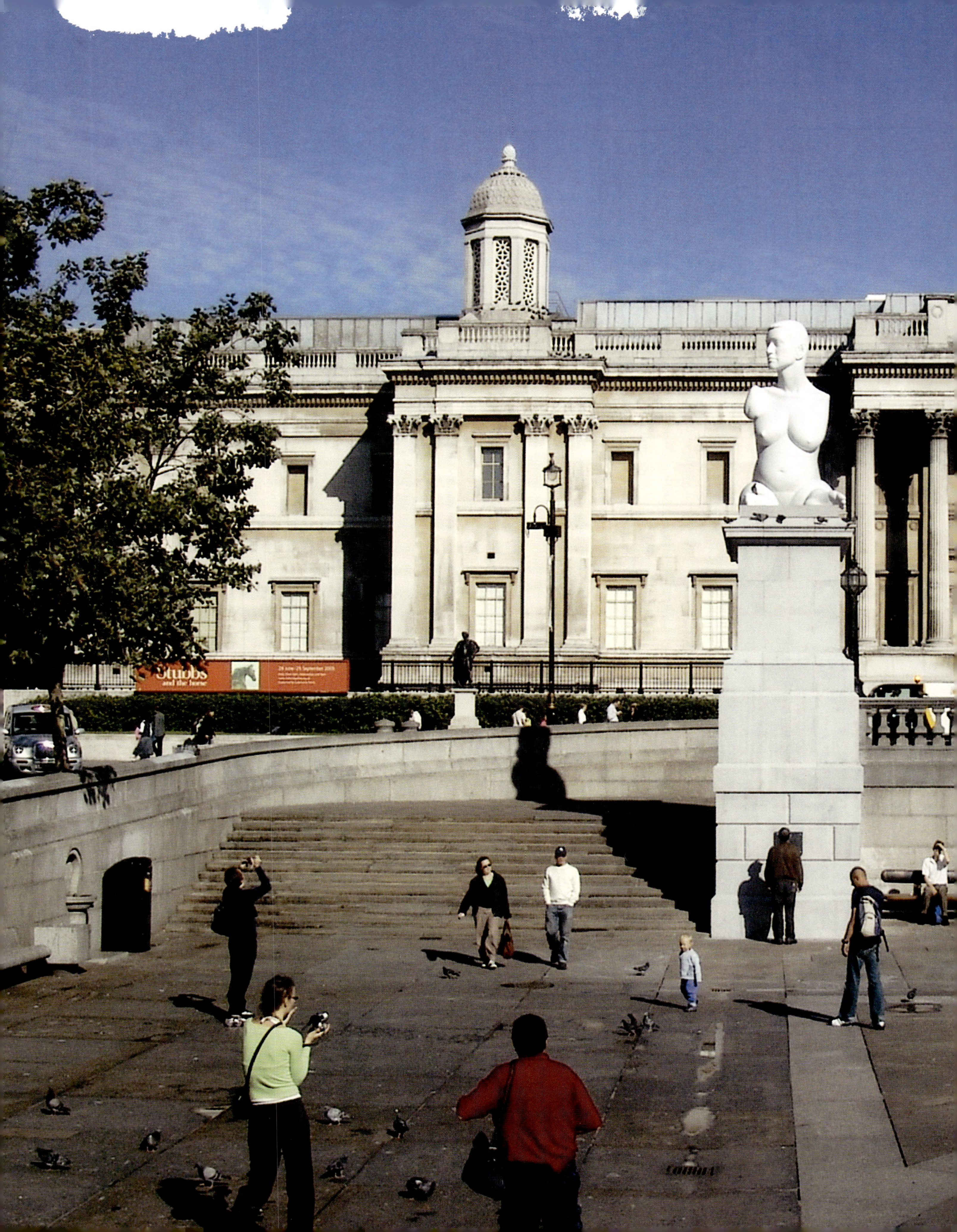

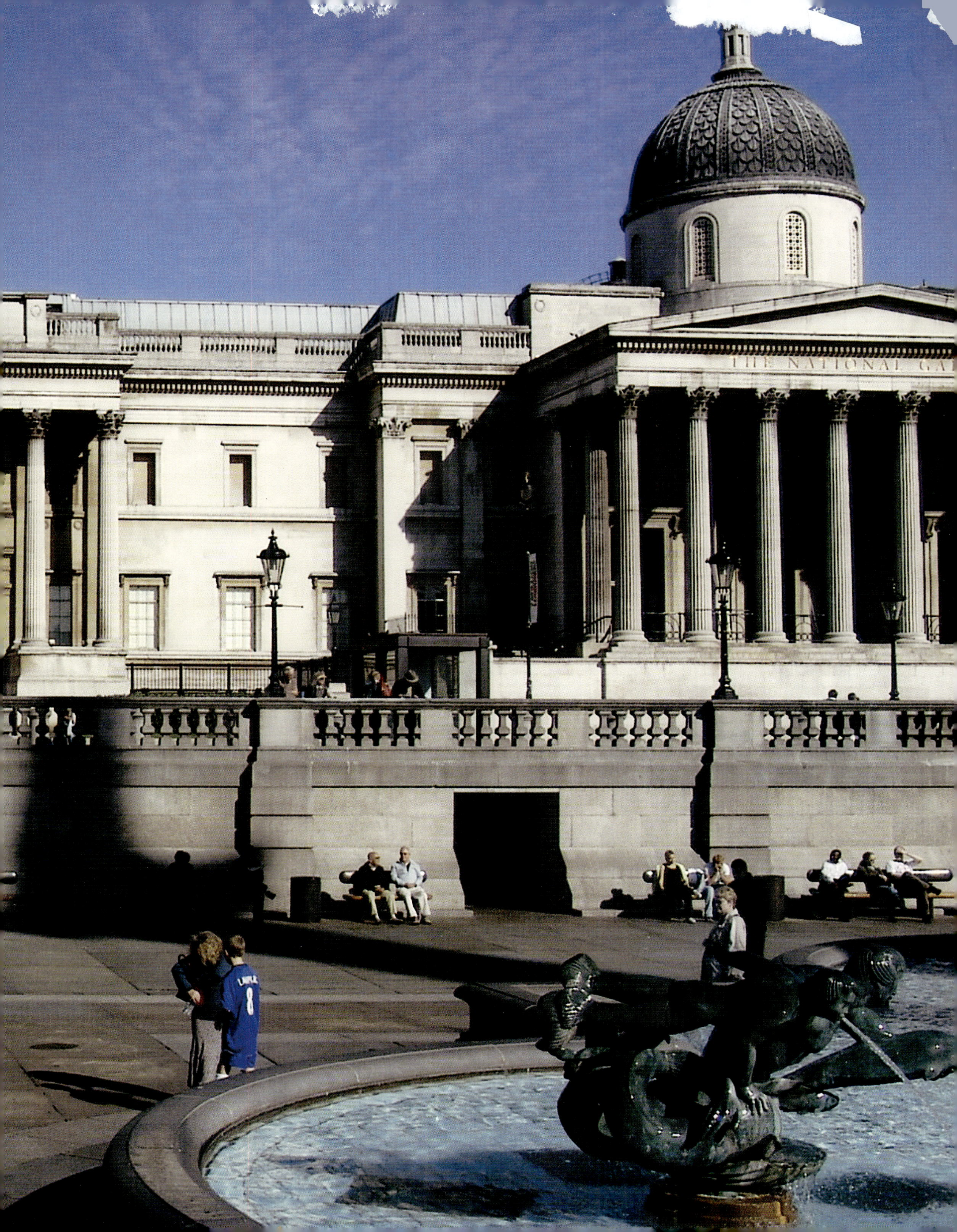
THE NATIONAL GA

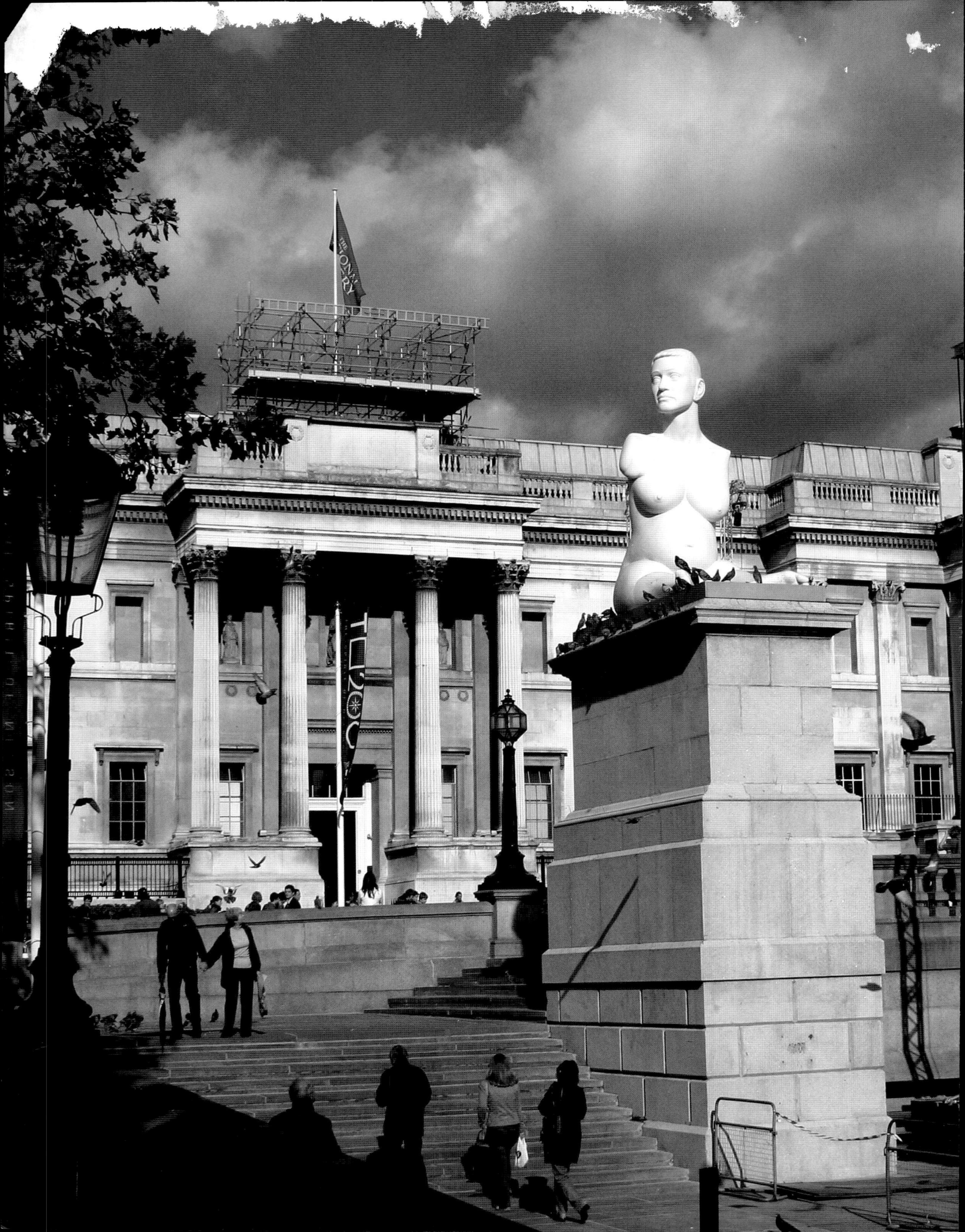

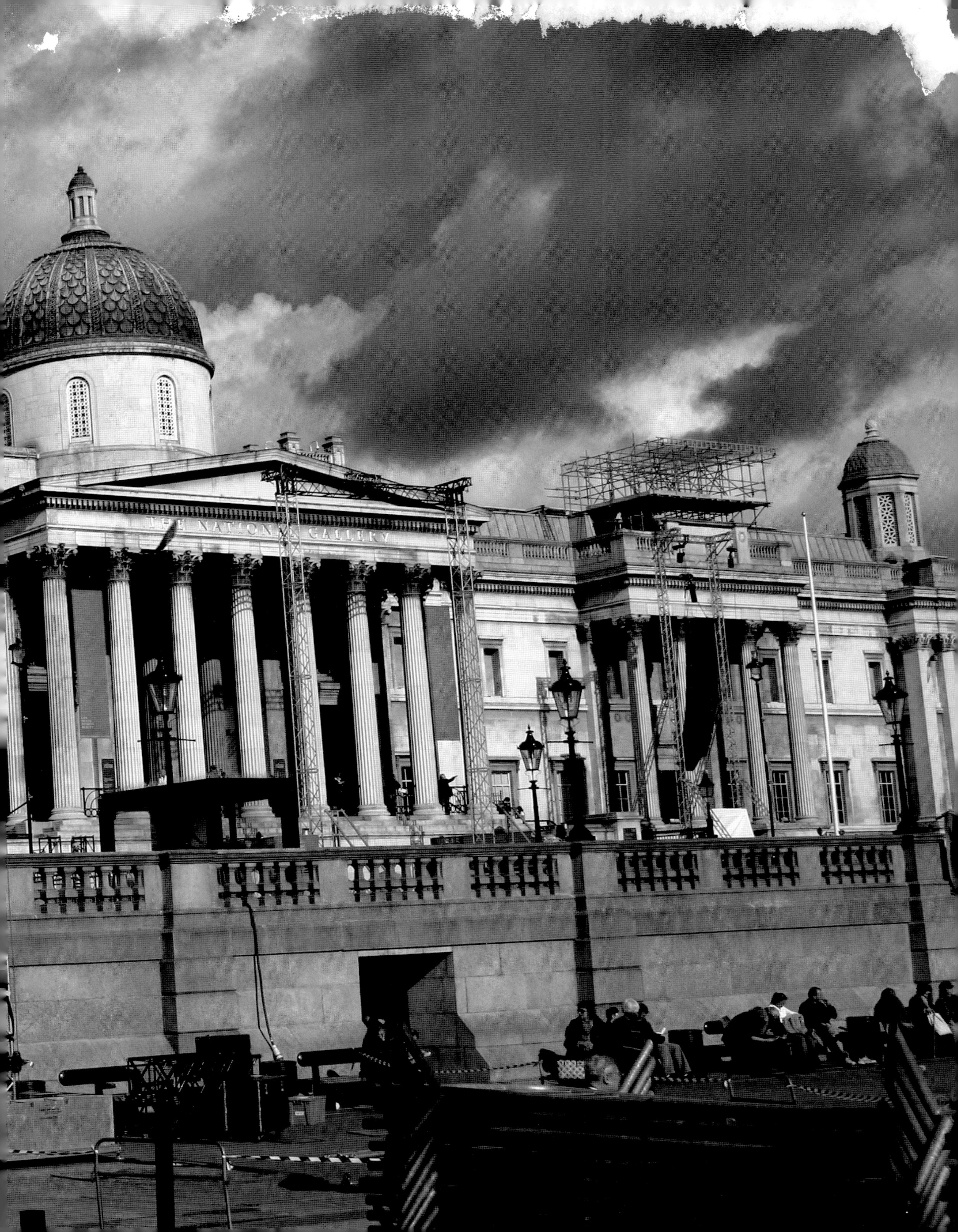
THE NATION
GALLERY

September 2005:
Media and public reaction following the installation of the sculpture on the Fourth Plinth

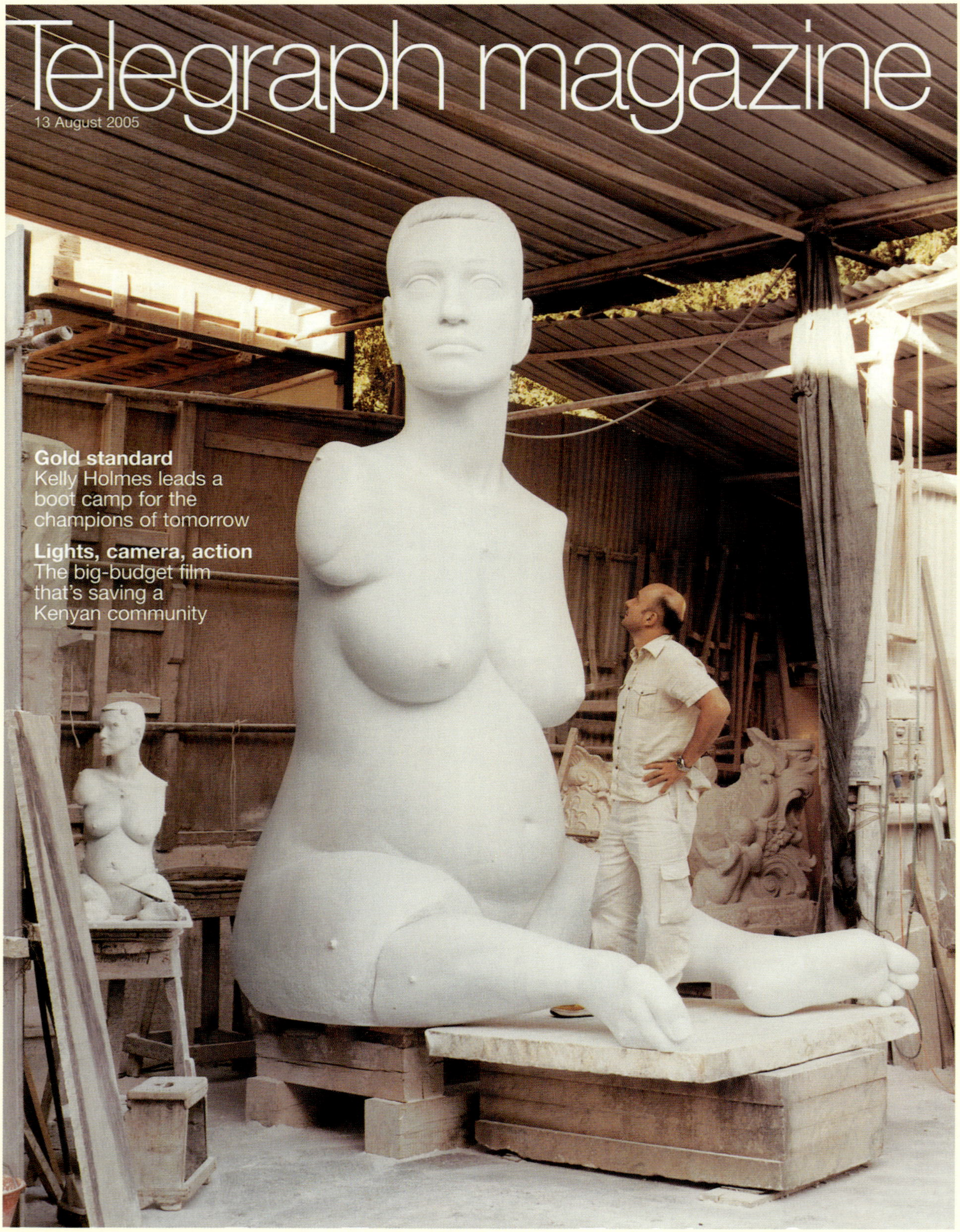

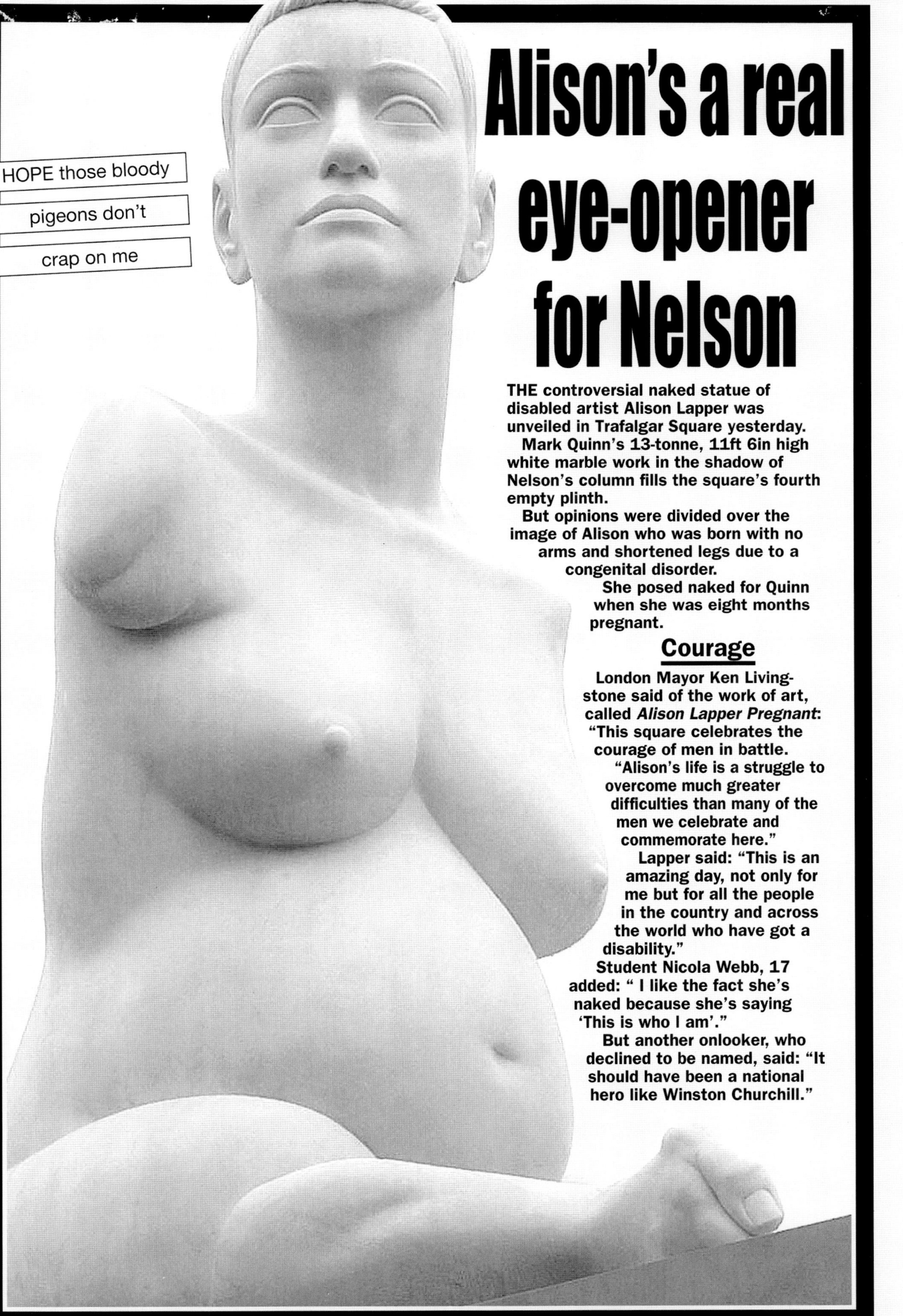

HOPE those bloody
pigeons don't
crap on me

Alison's a real eye-opener for Nelson

THE controversial naked statue of disabled artist Alison Lapper was unveiled in Trafalgar Square yesterday.

Mark Quinn's 13-tonne, 11ft 6in high white marble work in the shadow of Nelson's column fills the square's fourth empty plinth.

But opinions were divided over the image of Alison who was born with no arms and shortened legs due to a congenital disorder.

She posed naked for Quinn when she was eight months pregnant.

Courage

London Mayor Ken Livingstone said of the work of art, called *Alison Lapper Pregnant*: "This square celebrates the courage of men in battle.

"Alison's life is a struggle to overcome much greater difficulties than many of the men we celebrate and commemorate here."

Lapper said: "This is an amazing day, not only for me but for all the people in the country and across the world who have got a disability."

Student Nicola Webb, 17 added: " I like the fact she's naked because she's saying 'This is who I am'."

But another onlooker, who declined to be named, said: "It should have been a national hero like Winston Churchill."

New icon takes a seat in Trafalgar Square

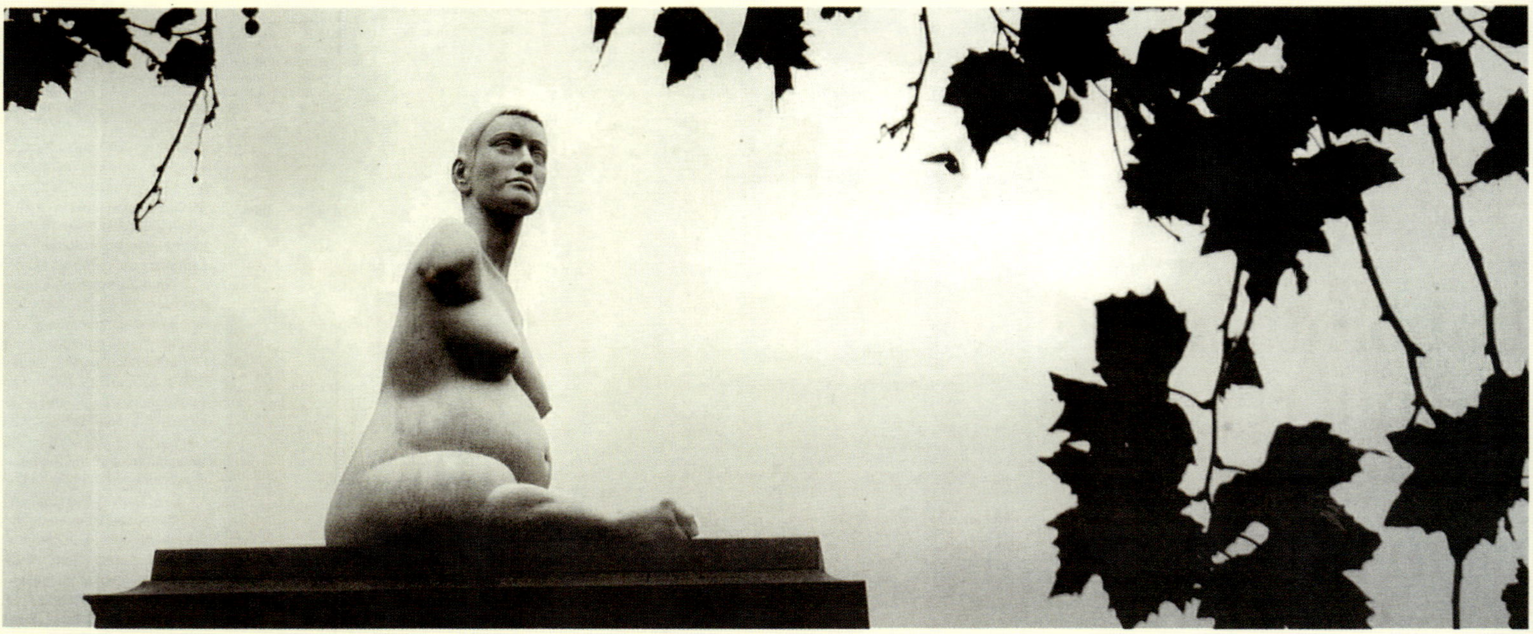

Marc Quinn's *Alison Lapper Pregnant* on the fourth plinth in Trafalgar Square; below, Alison Lapper and her son DAVID SANDISON

By Louise Jury
Arts Correspondent

Under the stony gaze of Lord Nelson and to the fascination of a rain-defying crowd, one of the most controversial pieces of public art in Britain has been unveiled.

Alison Lapper Pregnant, a 12-ton marble sculpture of a disabled woman eight months pregnant by the artist Marc Quinn, was installed on the fourth plinth of Trafalgar Square 18 months after it was chosen from a shortlist of six artists.

A guest at yesterday's ceremony, Lapper, 40, an artist, said she thought it was amazing, but not because it was her. "It's inspirational. It puts disability and femininity and motherhood on the map," she said. "It's time to challenge people's perceptions about these things. I'm hopeful it can make a difference."

In a reference to the military heroes on the other plinths, she added: "At least I didn't get here by slaying people."

The unveiling was the culmination of a process that began seven years ago when the cook Prue Leith, as deputy chairman of the Royal Society of Arts (RSA), began a debate on what should happen to the plinth. It was designed in 1841 to display an equestrian statue, but insufficient funds for the project meant it lay empty for a century and a half. Thanks to Ms Leith, the RSA installed three temporary sculptures, prompting the Government to set up a committee to ponder its future. It was recommended that the plinth should be used for an ongoing series of temporary works of art, and the mission fell to Ken Livingstone when he became Mayor of London.

He was triumphant yesterday as the 12ft sculpture, carved in white marble from Quinn's cast in Pietrasanta, Italy, took its place at last. "When we launched this project, it was either ignored or

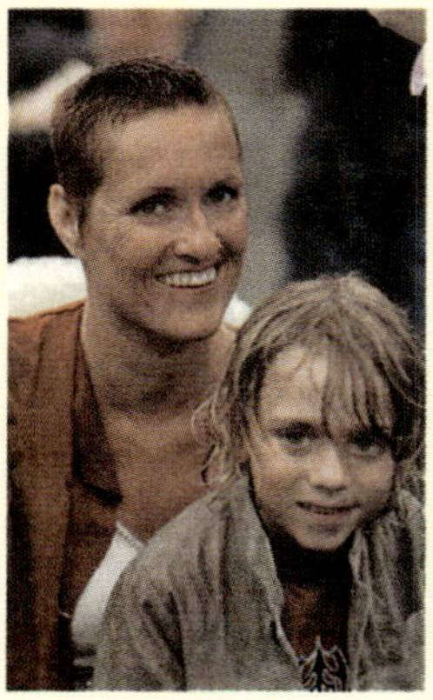

the reaction was hostile. Now everyone thinks it's great," he said. "This is a work about courage, beauty and defiance, which represents all that is best about our great city. *Alison Lapper Pregnant* is a modern heroine – strong, formidable and full of hope."

The statue will remain in Trafalgar Square for 18 months, followed in April 2007 by Thomas Schutte's *Hotel for the Birds*, another work from the shortlist.

Alison Lapper Pregnant will then be available for sale at a price of £500,000 in an edition of three. Funding of £180,000 from the Mayor and the Arts Council of England, which underwrote the project, will be reimbursed by the sale. But Quinn hoped that at least one would be bought for permanent display. "It's a public sculpture, I'd like it to stay public," he said.

His original inspiration was seeing old sculptures in the British Museum and deciding that if a real person with similar missing limbs were to arrive, museum visitors would be horrified.

"I realised there was no positive representation of disability in the history of public art," he said. But it was not a straightforward "message piece of art," he added. "To me, art is when you create space where meaning can occur."

LEADING ARTICLE, PAGE 34

... but what do artists and the

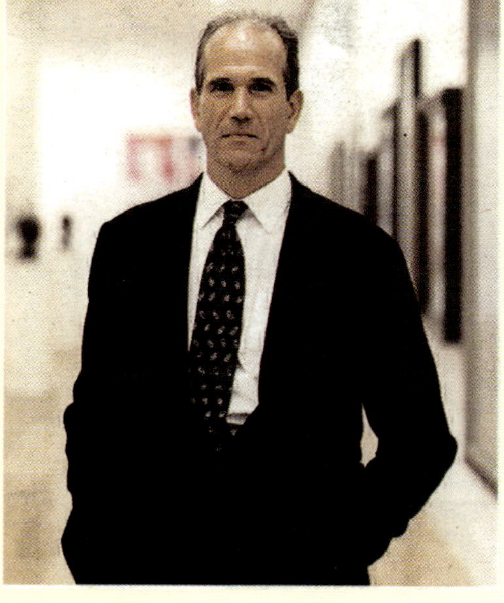

Sandy Nairne, director of the National Portrait Gallery and chair of the Fourth Plinth Commissioning Group
"We've got an even greater sculpture than I expected. The transfer from maquette to sculpture is a step-change not just in terms of scale but in the fineness of the carving and the fineness of the proportions. It's an important piece because it's both about ideas and about a person. It can provoke thought about Trafalgar Square, about history, but it's also about this extraordinary and fascinating person, Alison Lapper. I hope it improves the quality of the debate about contemporary public art."

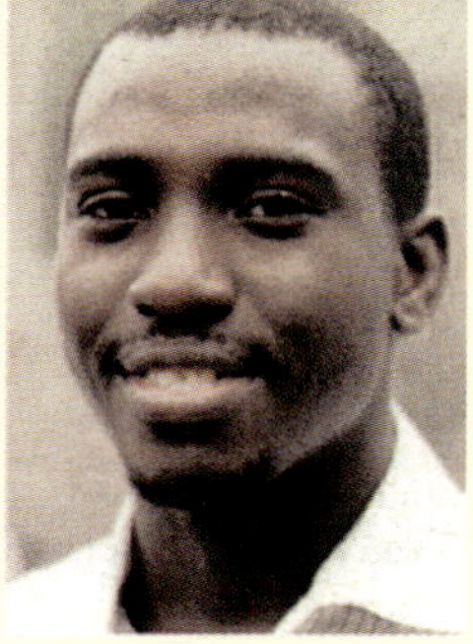

Obinna Onyekwe
MSc student of publ
health in London
"We've just arrived from Nigeria yester for me to study and saw it on the televis this morning and sa we had to come to s I like the fact that disabled people are represented, that d her disability she is there. I can't wait to a picture of it."

ublic think?

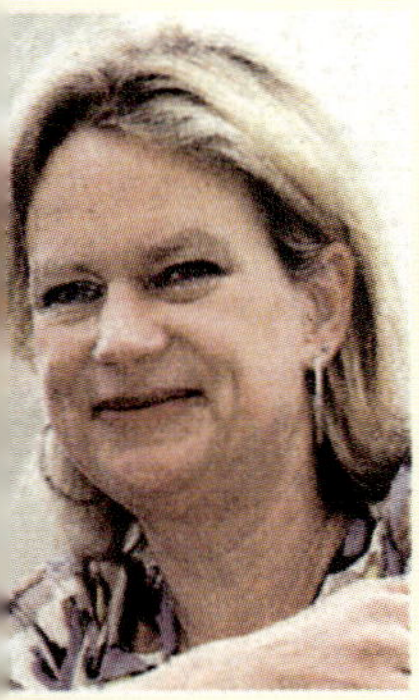

Louisa Buck, critic and 2005 Turner Prize judge
"The best public art has to focus debate and make people question how they look at art and why. Otherwise art just becomes part of the furniture – things like, that horrible phrase, 'the turd in the plaza' or that are just decorative. It's a great subject to have in this historical, phallic, male hero-dominated square."

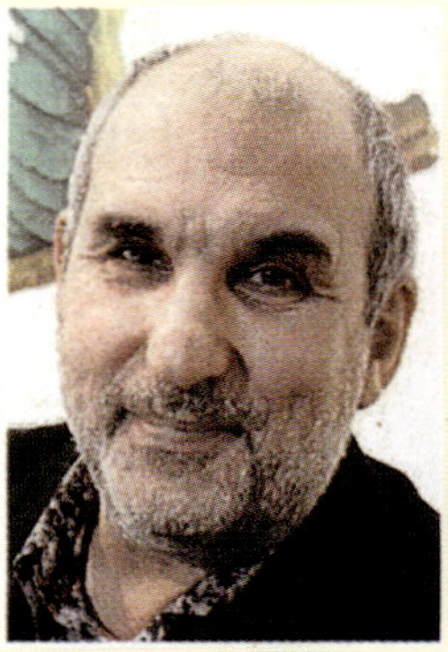

Alan Yentob, BBC's director of drama, entertainment and CBBC
"I like it. What is interesting is there are a whole lot of issues that this raises, such as what are monuments for, what about public sculpture? It opens up a debate about what art is, and whether you like it or don't like it, that is a very interesting dialogue. Look at old Nelson up there, he's got his back to it. He clearly doesn't like being upstaged."

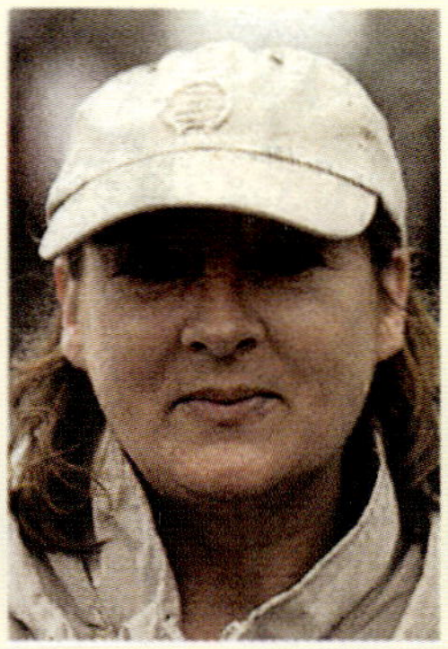

Penny Toyer, 42, a supermarket duty manager from Bournemouth
"I don't particularly like it. It's not very flattering, it's unfair on her. We saw a programme on TV about her and thought we would come to see it, but I don't think it's beautiful at all. I would have liked something a bit more feminine. You wouldn't know it was a lady, facially. But I think it's a good idea to change the statue every couple of years."

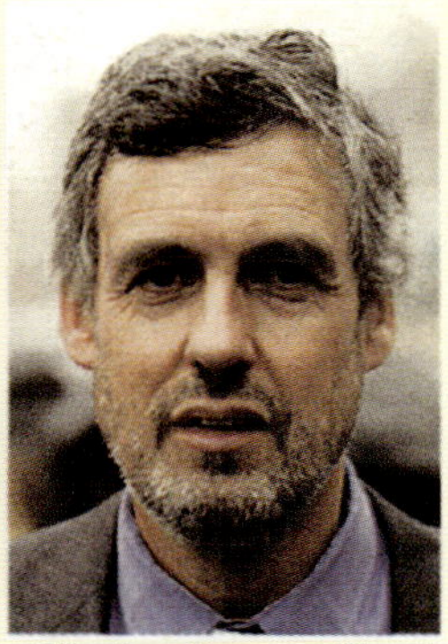

Stephen Green, national director Christian Voice
"We've got three plinths with military leaders and the only ones we have today are in the Ministry of Defence sacking people. So I think we should have [Alison Lapper] but it would have been better to do a statue of her with her kit on. It's a pity he had to do an indecent statue. She has her breasts and other bits hanging out. We need more modesty in our nation, not less."

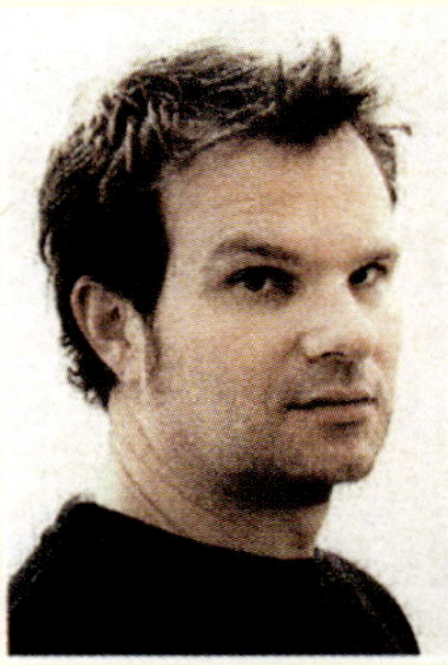

Martin Maloney, artist who has exhibited in shows including Sensation
"The scale is perfect, it's very simple. I think it's hard to make a piece of public sculpture because there are so many distractions in the outside world, but I think he's really pulled it off. You feel it's beautiful against the sky but also confrontational. It also makes me think of all the other classical sculptures that don't have arms."

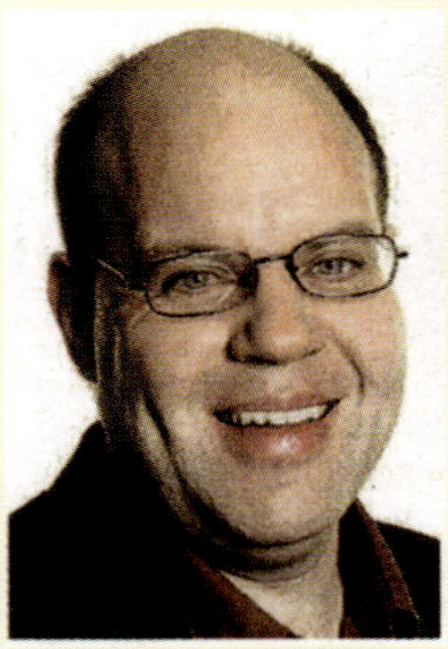

Mark Lawson, writer and broadcaster
"I had no sense of the scale of it. I hadn't imagined it would be that big. Marc Quinn has always drawn on the classical tradition in his art and he clearly has here. It's very noble. The crowd here seem to have backed it. There weren't as many people talking about it as there were talking about the cricket but people clearly were engaged in what should be there."

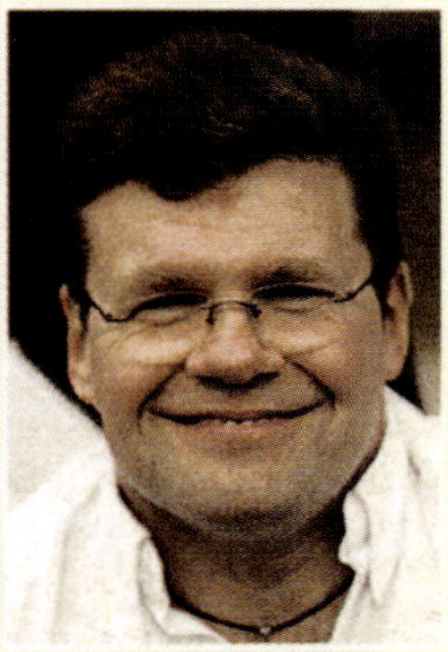

Peter Hull, disability sports development officer, 39, from Southampton who was born without legs and with short arms
"I've known Alison nearly 40 years. Everyone is different but her diversity stands out more. Whatever we look like, we can still be beautiful to someone. This celebrates the diversity of humans. On the other plinths are men of courage and she is courageous. The statue will make a difference."

On a pedestal, the Venus de Milo of the Square

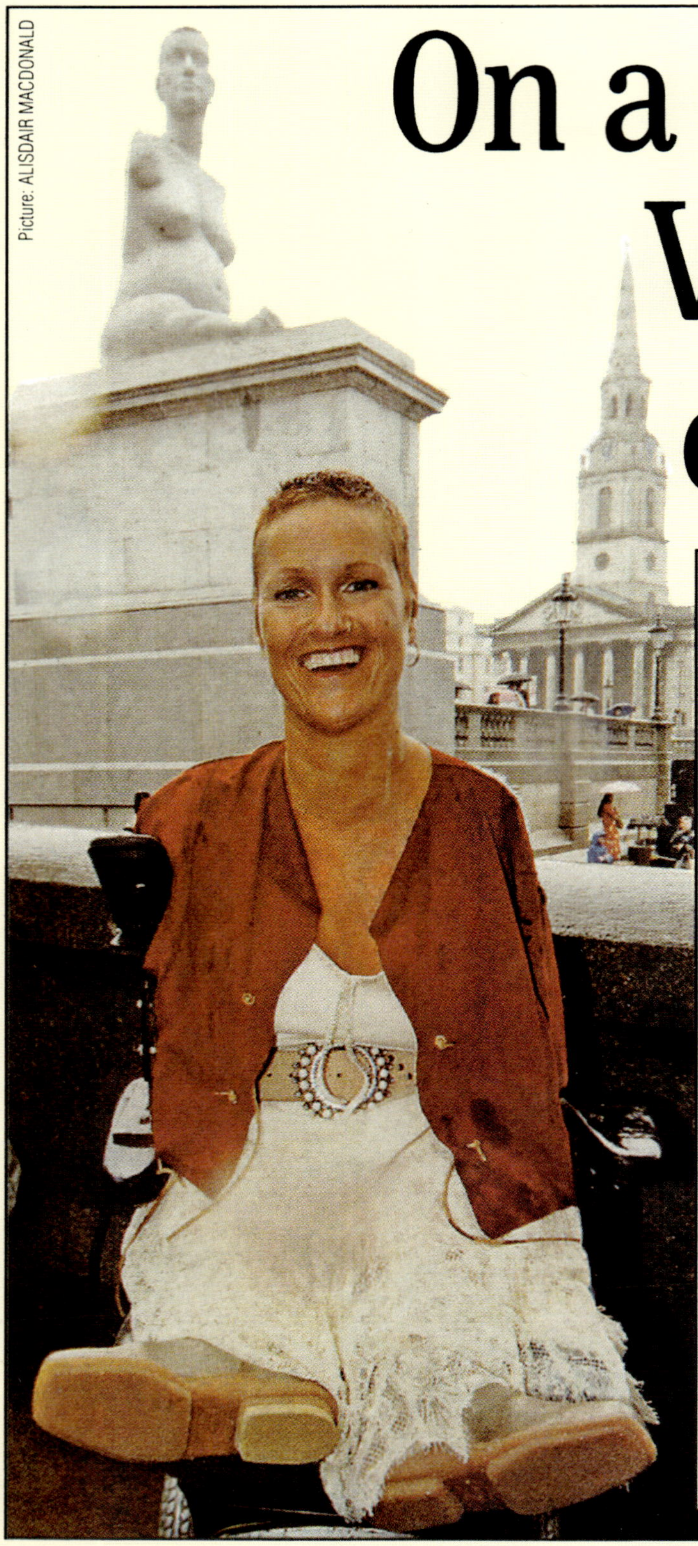

Picture: ALISDAIR MACDONALD

By **Geoff Marsh**

A STATUE of disabled artist Alison Lapper was officially unveiled in Trafalgar Square yesterday.

Mark Quinn's 13-ton, 11ft 6in high white marble sculpture of a pregnant woman is London's latest landmark.

Alison, who was born with no arms and shortened legs due to a congenital disorder, posed naked for Quinn when she was eight months pregnant.

London Mayor Ken Livingstone hailed her as a "modern heroine". He said the statue, titled Alison Lapper Pregnant, made a worthy companion to Nelson's Column.

"This square celebrates the courage of men in battle," said Mr Livingstone. "Alison's life is a struggle to overcome much greater difficulties than many of the men we celebrate and commemorate here."

Alison, who attended the unveiling ceremony with her five-year-old son Parys, said: "This is an amazing day not just for me, but for all the people in the country and across the world who have a disability."

The statue, which was welcomed by disability campaigners, will remain in the square for 18 months before being replaced by Thomas Schutte's Perspex installation, Hotel For The Birds.

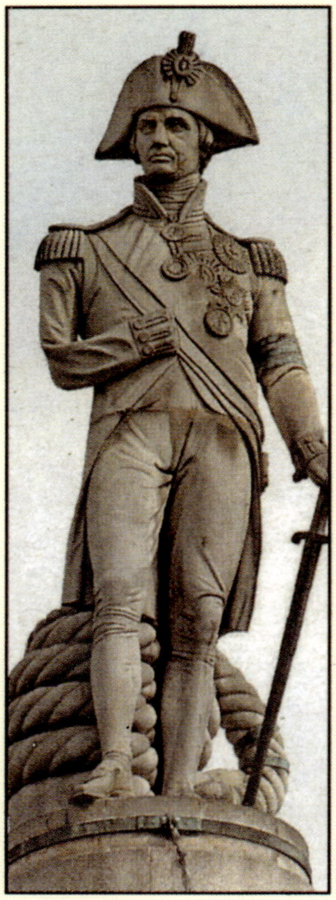

LANDMARK: Alison and statue, left. Above, Nelson

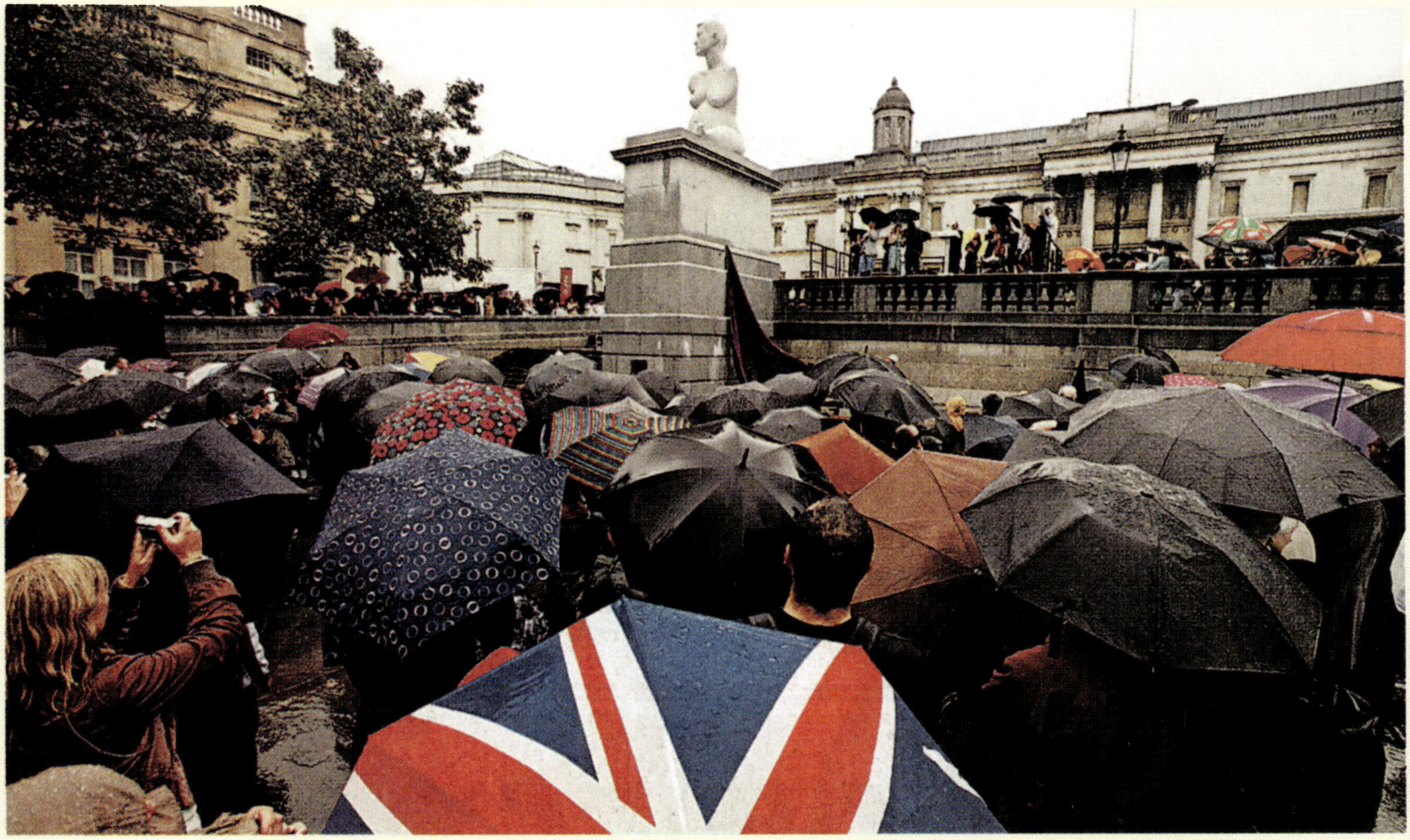

Marc Quinn's sculpture, Alison Lapper Pregnant, is unveiled in Trafalgar Square yesterday Photograph: Dan Chung

Expert view Adrian Searle

Arresting, strange and beautiful

Marc Quinn's Alison Lapper Pregnant is a much more arresting, impressive and strange work than photographs can convey. Even Alison Lapper's own naked, photographic self-portraits do not really prepare you for the sculpture itself.

Once seen, it is hard to drag one's eyes away. It isn't just the size and mass of Quinn's sculpture, or the cool, off-white marble, lighter than any of the stone of the square or the buildings around it. It is all in the form, and the strangeness of Alison Lapper's body itself, its irreducible familiarity and otherness. Necessarily, one struggles to describe her body in terms that do not make her sound grotesque – while even the medical name of her condition, phocomelia, refers to having limbs "like a seal's flipper". When the sculpture was installed, wrapped in polythene sheeting and tape, I thought of a Henry Moore wrapped by Christo. Unwrapped, she looks more like a sphynx by Odilon Redon, or a sculpture by Louise Bourgeois. One thinks of Jean Arp: but what one really thinks of is Alison Lapper.

Perhaps we needed the example of Picasso's portraits to recognise beauty in certain faces. And it could be that the model of Picasso's eroticised, biomorphic figures of the 1920s and 30s also allow us to see that Alison Lapper can be beautiful too, in the same way that Velasquez's portraits of dwarfs remind us of the humanity of his subjects.

Quinn's sculpture has nothing to do with the male heroics of Nelson and the generals on their plinths in the square. Lapper's supposed "heroism" is of an entirely different, deeper type. And in the end this is more sculpture than statuary. What is genuinely extraordinary about Marc Quinn's Alison Lapper Pregnant, is Alison Lapper, naked, pregnant.

Deborah Orr

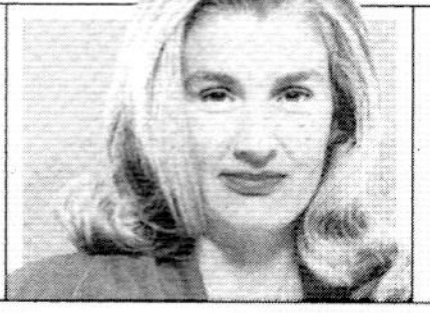

People love the statue, but would they coo at the image if it was on their scan?

I think it is fair to say that even the artist, Marc Quinn, was surprised by the magnitude of the physical presence exuded by his huge sculpture, *Alison Lapper Pregnant*. The statue, unveiled on Thursday on the fourth plinth in London's Trafalgar Square, effortlessly dominates its space. Its lightness of colour is so airy and its monumental size so substantial, that it manages to seem like a dream or a vision even as it sits there, calmly insistent, dominating all before, and behind, it. I'm already sad that it is meant to be there for only 18 months. It really ought to stay for good.

My enthusiasm isn't of the politically correct "mother courage" kind, either. The subject's gender (with nearly all human depictions in public statuary being of males), birth defect, her pregnancy, the reference of her missing marble limbs to classical sculpture's idealised beauty, all this, of course, brings visual interest, cultural content and social commentary to the piece.

Yet I find what seems like the most popular "intellectual" justification of the sculpture – that it displays a different, finer sort of courage than the admirals, knights, kings and lions already in the square – to be embarrassingly banal and cravenly self-conscious.

Yes, it took some guts for Alison Lapper to be cast naked and pregnant for Marc Quinn. But oddly, though Alison Lapper's own experience of life has been singular, the great thing about Marc Quinn's sculpture is that it says something wonderful about the human condition, in just the same way as Lapper herself does. This work is serious, yes. But it also makes your heart sing with joy.

Many people, including Lapper herself, consider the sculpture to have a political message. "People who are negative about the statues are the ones with a problem," she commented. "I think it gives a very powerful message about disability and motherhood and femininity and being a woman." This too, is true in as far as it goes. But my own view is that there are actually some rather unpleasant reasons why people might very much like the sculpture as well.

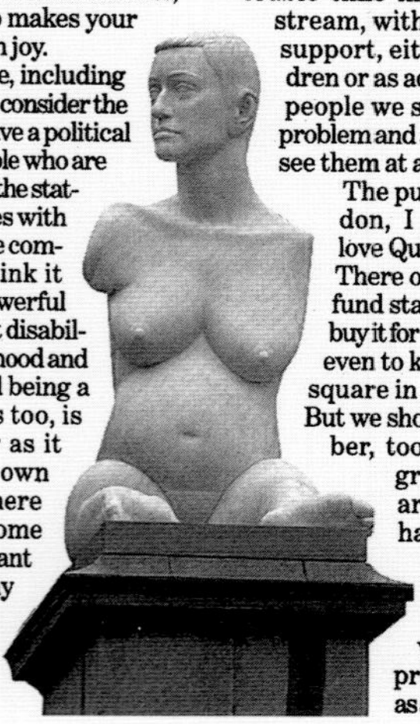

Chiefly, I think, the statue's existence there at the heart of the establishment, rendered in the medium favoured by Michelangelo, cooed over by people mithering on about Alison's own beauty and courage etc, is in some ways like much of the lip-service modern society pays to the idea of supporting the vulnerable. We can look at this statue and congratulate ourselves on our marvellous liberality and acceptance of people of all shapes and sizes, while at the same time forgetting that if we saw such an arresting image on our own ultrasound scan, we might not be quite so celebratory.

> Trouble is, not all disabled people are like Alison, and we still see them as a problem, if we see them at all

Alison Lapper was sent to a residential home for disabled children as a baby, which was an awful thing for her. Now, such places are being closed down, and the policy of "inclusion" dictates that all children must whenever possible be placed in mainstream education.

The trouble is that all disabled people are not Alison Lapper – brave and clever, brainy and stable, handsome and talented, passionate and vital. Many find it much harder to accept and be accepted, and they have a miserable time in the mainstream, without proper support, either as children or as adults. These people we still see as a problem and a drain, if we see them at all.

The public of London, I think, will love Quinn's statue. There ought to be a fund started now to buy it for London, and even to keep it in the square in perpetuity. But we should remember, too, that as a great piece of art the work has endless meaning, and that it is just as valid as a reproach as it is as a celebration.

DAVID Sullivan

SUNDAY SPORT PUBLISHER – The voice of common sense

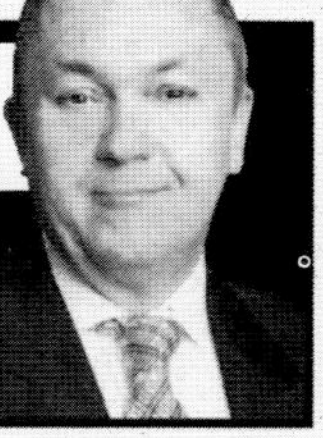

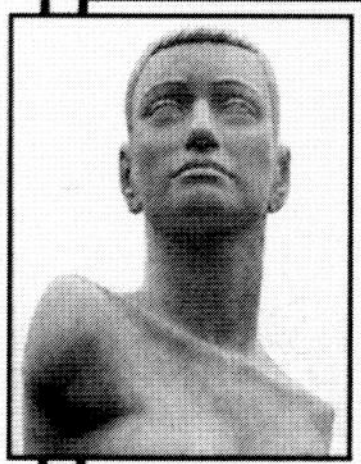

IT was an absolute delight to see the statue of disabled artist Alison Lapper unveiled in Trafalgar Square on Thursday.

The controversial work by Mark Quinn is a stunning piece of art and brings the Square into the modern age.

Tens of thousands of people pass Trafalgar Square every day without giving it so much as a second glance. The only people who take a look are tourists.

Now everyone is looking and thinking about the work. Everyone has an opinion — and that can only be a good thing.

Many want to preserve London as it has been for years, but the capital is a modern city which is always evolving.

To place a challenging work of art in such an iconic position in the capital shows that London is forward, not backward looking.

Well done to Ken Livingstone, the London Assembly, and everyone involved in the decision to place this statue in Trafalgar Square.

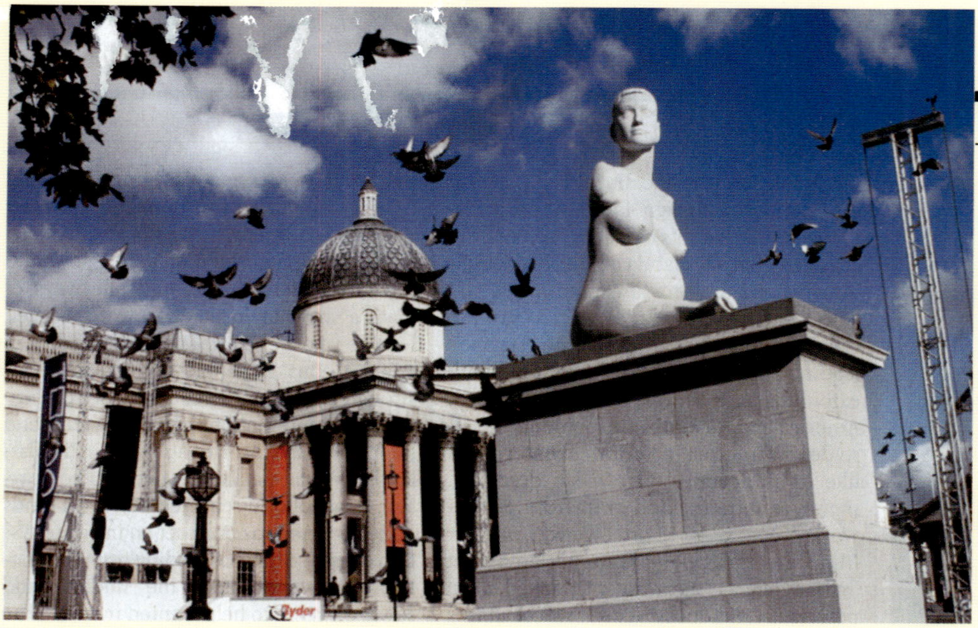

SOPHIA EVANS—NBPICTURES FOR TIME

MONUMENTAL Fans of the armless, pregnant, 12-metric-ton sculpture flock to see it

L E T T E R   F R O M   L O N D O N

Jumana Farouky

Rubbing Shoulders With Lord Nelson

A new addition to Trafalgar Square tests Londoners' capacity to be shocked

SHE'S HARD TO MISS. FIRST of all, she's huge—3.5 m tall, 12 metric tons. She's also naked. And eight months pregnant. Her legs are shrunken and twisted. She doesn't have any arms. Carved out of a single block of Italian marble, she's so white, she almost glows. But not everyone has quite got used to the pregnant, armless sculpture that has taken up residence in one of London's most trafficked public spaces, near monuments to the likes of Lord Nelson and King George IV. Sketching the statue for a class, Nisharee Pongpaew, 20, an art student from Brighton, registers her disapproval. "Around her are all these important people," says Pongpaew. "She's not a hero."

But maybe heroes aren't what they used to be. Since its unveiling last month, *Alison Lapper Pregnant*, a likeness of the disabled 40-year-old British artist and photographer Alison Lapper, has stirred debate across London, not just over the meaning of art but also about the city's evolving identity. To some, the sculpture's prominent display owes more to political correctness than to aesthetic merit—"Purely empty, deeply bland and silly," says art critic Matthew Collings, author of *This Is Modern Art*. Others call it an uplifting tribute to womankind. But more interesting than the reactions it provokes are the ones it doesn't. If the sculpture has met with less than universal acclaim, it has also failed to spark much outrage or spray-paint protest. In that sense, *Alison Lapper Pregnant* may reveal a city and a society more comfortable with itself than it has been for a long time.

Apart from a few recent temporary sculptures, the stone pedestal on the northwest corner of Trafalgar Square has stood empty since 1841. Londoners have long had their own ideas of what kind of statue should go on the plinth: Princess Diana! Margaret Thatcher! A giant pigeon! But lacking a permanent solution a government-appointed committee last year picked two works that would each occupy the spot for up to 18 months. Marc Quinn, 41, creator of *Alison Lapper Pregnant*, says he wanted his work to reflect classical influences while addressing a contemporary social issue. "Disabled people are largely underrepresented in the history of art," says Quinn. "I wanted to celebrate a different kind of beauty and bodily diversity."

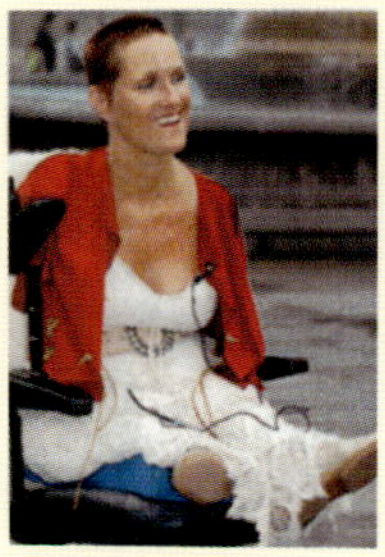

MICHAEL MELIA—RETNA

INSPIRATION Artist Alison Lapper poses near her marble likeness

It was hardly guaranteed that the sculpture would be deemed worthy of a place near Britain's greatest military heroes. But *Alison Lapper Pregnant* embodies the spirit of Trafalgar Square. For centuries, it has been the beating heart of the city, the place where Londoners gather to debate, celebrate and mourn. Only three months ago, people filled it to cheer the announcement that London will be host to the 2012 Olympics; eight days later, they flocked there again, to commemorate the July 7 terrorist bombings. Sandy Nairne, director of the National Portrait Gallery and chairman of the committee that chose the statue, says the judges wanted to honor the "demotic spirit" of the square as much as its history. *Alison Lapper Pregnant* fits right in: it's a monument to the strength of a human spirit, and it's impossible to ignore.

Londoners seem to appreciate the rebellious nature of Quinn's sculpture. "It's good to push minorities to the front of art," says Jon Bryan, 48, an unemployed Londoner who lost his right arm in a bicycle accident. Twenty years ago, it might have been a different story. During the late 1980s and '90s, a group of upstart conceptualists dubbed the Young British Artists sparked outrage by pushing the boundaries of taste and convention. (Quinn froze casts of his head filled with his own blood.) But as London became increasingly cosmopolitan, the public lost its capacity to be shocked. Says Nairne: "Now London has all these different points of view, and that produces discussion. It's part of the city's growing confidence."

The novelty of *Alison Lapper Pregnant* is already wearing off. The most attention she gets these days is from the pigeons that perch on her lap. It says something about London's acceptance of change that they will probably like the next sculpture just as much, especially since it's called *Hotel for the Birds*. ■

Heroes come in all shapes and sizes

DOWN in Trafalgar Square, Nelson and the other heroes of British military might have a new neighbour.

For previous Tony Parsons columns see our website at www.mirror.co.uk

A pregnant, naked, severely disabled woman.

Marc Quinn's massive sculpture, Alison Lapper Pregnant, depicts a woman who was born with no arms and truncated legs.

Carved from white Italian marble, the sculpture was made when Alison Lapper was heavily pregnant with her now six-year-old son.

The very idea of this sculpture sent blood pressures soaring across the nation. Politically correct! Self-indulgent! An insult to our national heritage!

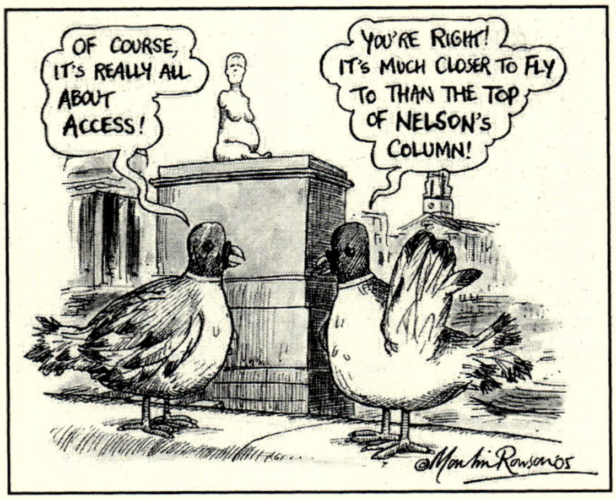

I wasn't too keen on the idea myself. It felt like all the advocates of Alison Lapper Pregnant, from Ken Livingstone on down, were the kind of people who despise our country's history. As a Horatio Nelson groupie, surely I would loathe this sculpture? But when you actually go down and see the statue, it takes your breath away.

Far from insulting Nelson and all those heroes you haven't actually heard of, Alison Lapper co-exists quite happily with them.

You need to see the statue with the clouds behind it, with the spray of the fountains in your face.

It moved me to tears.

Here is a Venus de Milo for our age. The statue is shocking and beautiful. Even if you know nothing about Alison Lapper – that she was taken away from her mother at birth, hidden away in an institution, and later abused – it is profoundly moving.

Here is an overwhelming sculpture of a woman who has had to fight every day of her life. Not better or worse than Nelson (with his one eye and his one arm) but different.

And a true British hero.

Alison Lapper Pregnant does what all great works of art should do.

It makes you think.

It makes you think about our concept of beauty. It makes you think about the very notion of heroism.

It makes you think about how we prefer the disabled to stay out of sight.

The statue is due to be taken down in 18 months.

They should keep it there for ever.

"Alison Lapper Pregnant," Marc Quinn's sculpture of his friend who was born with shortened legs and without arms, is to remain in Trafalgar Square until 2007.

In Trafalgar Square, Much Ado About Statuary

By SARAH LYALL

LONDON, Oct. 9 — The new statue was bound to make a vivid impression in Trafalgar Square, a place as redolent of past military glory as any in London. For one thing, it depicts someone who is not male, not wearing a uniform and not dead.

But there's more. The statue, 11 feet 7 inches of snow-white Carrara marble, shows the naked, eight-and-a-half-month-pregnant figure of 40-year-old Alison Lapper, a single mother who was born with shortened legs and no arms. Ms. Lapper is a friend of the sculptor, Marc Quinn, who has said that Nelson's Column, the focal point of Trafalgar Square, is "the epitome of a phallic male moment" and that he thought "the square needed some femininity."

But "Alison Lapper Pregnant" — juxtaposed as it is with the majestic figures of a king, two generals and the naval hero Lord Nelson — has fueled a sharp discussion here about art, the purpose of public monuments, and the appropriateness of displaying such a piece in such a singular public space.

It was commissioned early last year by a government-appointed panel that selects a rotating series of works for the long-empty plinth at the northwest corner of the square, a Mecca for tourists and art lovers next to the National Gallery. It was installed last month and is to be replaced in 2007 by Thomas Schütte's "Hotel for the Birds."

As they stroll around Trafalgar Square, passersby look at the statue of Ms. Lapper about as readily as they ignore the one of Sir Henry Havelock, a general who helped suppress the Indian rebellion of 1857. (He is also known for distributing Bibles to his troops.) If nothing else, the work succeeds — in the same way that Damien Hirst's shark-in-a-tank piece did in the early 1990's — because it is noticed and it gets people talking.

Some like it very much. "I like the concept of having a statue which represents the less-represented part of humanity," said Peter Waugh, 69, a retired teacher from Birmingham. "Lions are all right," he

Continued on Page 7

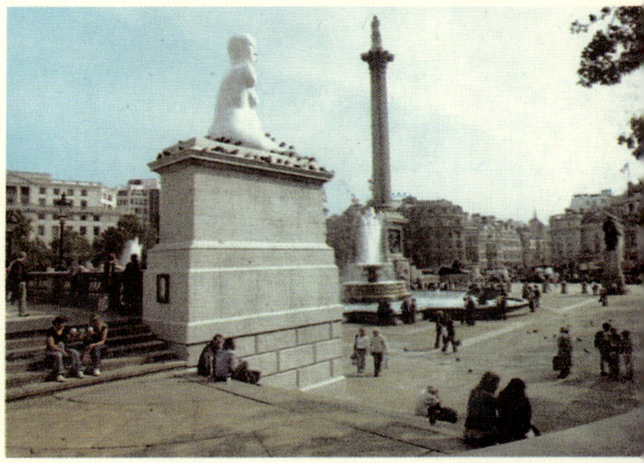

Jonathan Player for The New York Ti

The statue on its plinth. Mr. Quinn said he thought the square, dominated by a statue of Lord Nelson, "needed some femininity."

Bold, brave, beautiful

Marc Quinn's sculpture of Alison Lapper has completely transformed Trafalgar Square

RACHEL COOKE

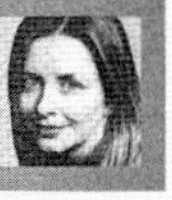

ALISON LAPPER PREGNANT Trafalgar Square, London WC2

I EXPECTED to be writing about how much I disliked *Alison Lapper Pregnant*, the 12-ton, marble sculpture that now graces Trafalgar Square's fourth plinth. I had seen pictures of Marc Quinn's maquette of the piece and had thought the subject matter – Lapper was born with no arms and shortened legs – too deliberately controversial, too feebly didactic and, as a result, rather banal.

But I should have known better. When it comes to sculpture, never underestimate the move from maquette to finished work. In the case of *Alison Lapper Pregnant*, something wonderful has happened in the zoom from miniature to massive, and it is not only the sheer scale of the thing (the statue is 3.55 metre tall and manages to feel even bigger) that demands a certain respect. White and dazzling, Quinn's sculpture has set a grey corner of a grey space unexpectedly ablaze.

On Thursday, when the piece was unveiled, it was raining: driving, dirty rain of a kind that always feels singular to London. Beyond all the umbrellas, mayor Ken was droning on; I couldn't catch what he was saying. *Alison Lapper Pregnant* was swathed in stately purple cloth, like a giant competitor in a wet T-shirt competition. Most people, I think, just wanted Ken to get on with it, so they could race home, or back to their offices, and wrap themselves in a towel.

But then the cloth came off and it was as if someone had switched on a light. Against a sky the colour of old underwear, a circle of buildings that might as well be built of concrete for all the life and warmth their stony facades exude, Quinn's womanly but warrior-like Lapper in marble from Pietrasanta, Italy, glowed like a beacon. Around me, the damp crowd started to smile and to talk.

Quinn says his inspiration came from the fact that there was 'no positive representation of disability in the history of public art'. Lapper says that she hopes the sculpture will 'make a difference... it's inspirational. It puts disability and femininity and motherhood on the map. It's time to challenge people's perceptions of these things. I'm hopeful it can make a difference'.

Looking at the statue, I wondered whether she might not be right about this. I hate overt messages in art, which is why my favourite of all the pieces that have graced the fourth plinth is still Rachel Whiteread's wonderfully sly and elusive *Monument*.

But what strikes you about *Alison Lapper Pregnant* are its elegant proportions, the implacable rightness of the way his subject sits there. It brings to mind the classical statues that grace our greatest museums, other sculptures from other times which also have, whether by accident or design, missing arms and legs.

YOU LOOK AT HER FACE AND HER SWOLLEN BELLY, AND ONLY LATER DO YOU WONDER ABOUT HER LIMBS

Quinn's sculpture is very beautiful, and this is how it works on you, in insidious fashion. Lapper has written a book about her life, and knowing the details – that her mother periodically abandoned her; that she is now a feisty single mother – remind you of all that she has struggled against, of how vivid and extraordinary a person she must be.

But I don't think they come in to play as you gaze on her outsize image in Trafalgar Square, though as a fighter, she takes her rightful place alongside the soldiers on the other plinths, Charles Napier and Henry Havelock. No, by choosing to portray Lapper naked and pregnant, Quinn has given us an Everywoman. You look at her face, her breasts and her swollen belly, and only afterwards do you wonder about her limbs.

Alison Lapper Pregnant will be in situ for 18 months, when it will be replaced by Thomas Schutte's *Hotel for the Birds*. I hope this cycle of change continues for a very long time to come (the fourth plinth, designed by Charles Barry, was built in 1841; the funds to top it with an equestrian statue never materialised).

The arrival of Quinn's sculpture is an event, one that, through sheer verve and loveliness alone, seems to knock into a cocked hat the tired debate about what constitutes public art. *This* is public art, and let that be an end of it.

I would like to think that the plinth commissions will become a regular excitement, just like Tate

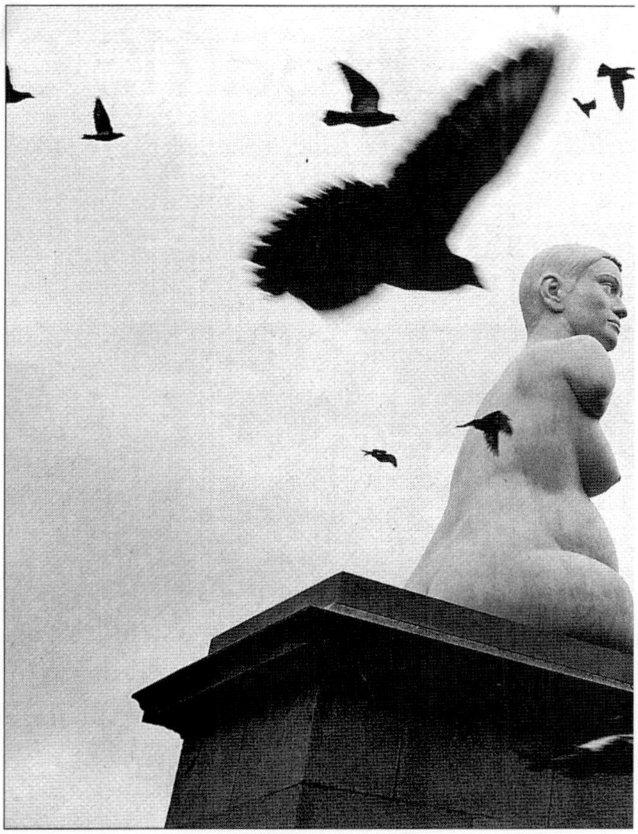

Pigeons fly past Marc Quinn's 'warrior-like' marble statue. Photograph by Dan Chung

POWERFUL PRESENCE: FIRST IMPRESSIONS IN TRAFALGAR

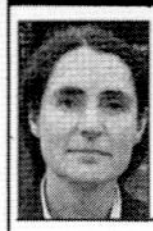

MARIA CLERKIN OFFICE MANAGER South-east London

It's just a beautiful statue and I don't think it's offensive at all. The stone really draws you to it, doesn't it? After all, it's certainly a nice change from all the generals.

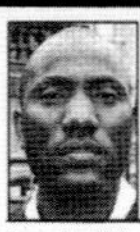

LEIKAN DIABIRI BANKER Nigeria

Lovely. It's just lovely. I don't know what it's supposed to symbolise, but it really leaves an impression.

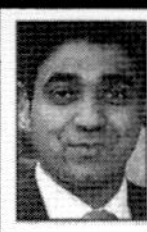

MOHAMMED CHOWHURY ACCOUNTANT Manor Park, London

It's a good statue in the way that it's a symbol of women, but it doesn't fit. It shouldn't be here. Trafalgar Square is a place of history; this isn't. But the statue itself is inspiring to disabled women. It's full of respect.

8 MARC QUINN, *ALISON LAPPER PREGNANT* (TRAFALGAR SQUARE, LONDON) Asked to place a temporary sculpture on Trafalgar Square's empty Fourth Plinth, Quinn chose to counter Britain's military heroes with a nearly-twelve-foot-tall naked woman carved from white marble—a portrait of Alison Lapper, herself an artist. She is not only eight months pregnant, but deformed due to a chromosomal defect that robbed her of arms and stunted her legs. A startling transgression for public sculpture, she presides here, seated, with grave dignity as a new kind of earth mother forcing us to rethink our ingrained prejudices about human beings who don't measure up to the macho standards of Lord Nelson, who, standing, still reigns aloft on a megacolumn. (Incidentally, he, too, was missing an arm.)

nents by
mbers of the Public

'It's a nice sculpture, it's quite personal — I like the fact she's naked because she's saying "this is who I am". And it's about time there was a statue of a woman here.'
Nicola Webb, 17, a student from Walthamstow, east London

'I don't see why a disabled person shouldn't be here — we all have to think about these things, don't we?' There's that one in Rome with no arms and everybody likes that one. It's a bit upsetting in a way. It's sad to think someone has to go through what she's gone through, but if she doesn't mind it then why should we?'
Molly Sinclair, 77, from Streatham, south London

'Everyone is looking at it saying they think it's wonderful but it's the Emperor's New Clothes. I don't object to having a disabled person up there and the statue itself is very well done, but who is she? They could have chosen someone much better who everyone has heard of. I'd prefer to see a great British comedian up there like Tommy Cooper or Eric Morecambe. At least it would give people a laugh.'
Philip Brannon, 63, from Croydon, south London

'I know you're not supposed to say it these days but I don't want to look at something like that. I'm sure there's a place for a disabled statue but I don't think it's appropriate in Trafalgar Square. It should have been a national hero like Winston Churchill.'
Anonymus

'I think the statue is brilliant. Disability is something which shouldn't be hidden away or be ashamed of. Good for Alison. Shame on all those people who are against it. Perhaps they should open their eyes.'
Bridget, Chatham, England

'The statue itself is largely irrelevant, as a piece of art it is mediocre at best. What is relevant is the location. This spot should have been used to display an individual who has done great deeds for the country, a British hero. Which, with the greatest of respect, the current subject is not. Whoever made this decision is being controversial for controversy's sake and should be roundly condemned.'
Tom, Edinburgh, Scotland

'Obviously everybody is entitled to their opinion but I disagree with those who criticise the choice. I think it's a wonderful piece. It says so much about so many people and it also shows that life goes on.'
Iain, Barnes, London

'I think it's a beautiful sculpture that inspires thinking and may just inspire others to open their minds and accept that being disabled doesn't mean you should be disqualified, even from art. This sculpture is of life overcoming all the odds.'
J. Kiros, Houston, TX

'The work is bourgeois and parochial. The subject is held up by the artist as a stick with which to beat the supposedly ignorant masses. I've never seen a more dull or moralising piece of work, it is indicative of a severe lack of artistic imagination and creativity'.
Burner, UK

'OK for an art gallery but not for a public square.'
William Howe, London

'I think it is great. For too long Trafalgar Square has been linked to the taking of life and war. It is good to see a statue of someone waiting to have a baby — bringing life not taking it!! Long may it remain.'
Andrew, Birmingham

'It's wonderful to see an image of a strong, beautiful woman being given the attention it deserves, for once. Disability disregarded, the UK's young women have a great role model in Ms Lapper, and for that alone I'd like to see her statue find a permanent spot somewhere in my home city.'
Rebecca Young, expat Londoner, Manchester, UK

'Why does the only statue of a woman in the square have to be so weak and dependant — naked and heavily pregnant? There are plenty of women who went into making this country great and deserve to be represented next to the military greats — the suffragettes for a start.'
A. Barnett, London, UK

'I thoroughly agree with all those who commissioned this piece of art. It's beautiful, it's based on a truly inspiring woman, and it represents women, disability and motherhood. What more could you ask for?'
Heather Grant, London

'Any criticism of execution of this statue is redundant – it is about the subject. It should be there permanently, to remind the majority non-disabled public that we are people as much as they are. No-one decries the Venus de Milo, a statue Alison has also imitated in her own work, so why decry this?'
Chris Page, Letchworth, UK

'Congratulations on whoever decided to take this decision. How refreshing to see a disabled person just getting on with life. I think this statue will show the able bodied that disability does not mean you can't live a full and rewarding life.'
Simon Brooks, Hatfield

'I have seen a recent documentary about Alison and her life and her courage, which I have to say amazes me. How many other people would have coped with her disability in the same way? Not many I reckon. Well done to Alison's sculpture, her guts and determination could shame us all.'
Carol Ferrie, Alexandria

'I think the artist may have failed to notice that the central figure in Trafalgar Square is a sculpture of a disabled person. Under-represented?'
Jake Wagg, Wantage, UK

'The statue doesn't do justice to the subject and has little sympathy for its surroundings – thankfully it's not a permanent fixture!'
Duncan, Oxford, UK

'I find its location totally inappropriate for Trafalgar Square. The square is dedicated to a disabled Naval captain who saved Britain from invasion. No offence, but what has Alison done for the country?'
Andy, UK

'If it's getting people hot under the collar, then it's doing exactly what art ought to do. Too many politicians and ordinary folk are scared to confront the extraordinary, and the intelligent should be happy to be taken out of their "comfort zones". Congratulations to those brave enough to challenge us.'
David Harper, Bradford, Yorkshire

'I think it is fantastic. While women are under-represented in terms of statues around Great Britain, disabled people are swept under the carpet and forgotten. The only figures we seem to celebrate are male and have a military background! For once let's celebrate a woman for whom every day tasks are a battle. Alison should be very, very proud.'
Kate, London

'I don't have a great problem with it. But people who accuse the new statue of being 'political' must also accept the fact that Trafalgar Square itself was an entirely political idea.'
Will Parker, Newport, South Wales

'I've nothing against Alison Lapper, but the statue is in the most inappropriate place. Trafalgar Square is for what it's meant, to commemorate the Battle of Trafalgar. In this particular year, there's only one candidate for the fourth plinth... Vice Admiral Collingwood, who was Nelson's second in command. But if you want to bring anybody's attention to the plight of the disabled, and how they cope with their disability, who better than Nelson himself to put over the message?'
G. Ireland, Birkenhead, UK

'All involved in this project should be applauded. Wonderful!'
Steve Clarke, Nether Stowey, Bridgwater, Somerset

'I think it's fantastic – a beautiful sculpture of a beautiful woman – an image always worthy of celebration.'
Jo, Kent

'I think it is grotesque. This is not meant as a slur on Alison, but on the piece of work itself.'
Rita Hollis, Shepton Mallet, Great Britain

phy

1964 Born, London
1985 Graduated, Cambridge University

Currently lives and works in London

Solo Exhibitions

2005 *Fourth Plinth*, Trafalgar Square, London
Chemical Life Support, White Cube, London
Meat Sculptures, Mary Boone Gallery, New York

2004 *The Incredible World of Desire*, IBM Building, New York
Marc Quinn, Atkinson Gallery, Millfield School, Somerset
The Overwhelming World of Desire (Paphiopedilum Winston Churchill Hybrid), Tate Britain, London
Flesh, Irish Museum of Modern Art, Dublin
The Complete Marbles, Mary Boone Gallery, New York

2003 *The Overwhelming World of Desire (Phragmipedium Sedenii)*, Peggy Guggenheim Collection, Venice
Mirror, A Delta Axis Initiative, Power House, Memphis
The Overwhelming World of Desire (Paphiopedilum Winston Churchill Hybrid), Goodwood Sculpture Park, West Sussex

2002 *Behind the Mask: Portraits*, Hatton Gallery, Newcastle
1+1=3 (Rainbow Sculpture), Cammell Laird Ship Yard, Liverpool
Italian Landscapes from Garden 2000, Terrace Gallery Harewood, Leeds
Marc Quinn, Tate Liverpool, Liverpool

2001 *A Genomic Portrait. John Sulston by Marc Quinn*, National Portrait Gallery, London
Marc Quinn. Garden, Art of this Century, Paris
Italian Landscape, Habitat, London

2000 *Still Life*, White Cube, London
Marc Quinn, Groninger Museum, Groningen
Marc Quinn, Fondazione Prada, Milan

1999 *Marc Quinn*, Kunstverein Hannover, Hannover
Marc Quinn. Drawings, Sala Amárica-Amarica Aretoa, Vitoria

1998 *Incarnate*, Gagosian Gallery, New York
Marc Quinn, South London Gallery, London

1997 *Infra-slim Spaces*, Invisible Museum, SCCA, Kiev

1995 *The Blind Leading the Blind*, Jay Jopling/White Cube, London
Emotional Detox: The Seven Deadly Sins. Art Now, Tate Gallery, London

1994 *Marc Quinn*, Jay Jopling/Art Hotel, Amsterdam

1993 *Marc Quinn*, Galerie Jean Bernier, Athens

1991 *Out of Time*, Jay Jopling/Grob Gallery, London

1990 *Bread Sculpture*, Galerie Marquardt, Paris
Bread Sculpture, Middendorf Gallery, Washington

1988 *Bronze Sculpture*, Jay Jopling/Otis Gallery, London

Group Exhibitions

2005 *Art Out of Place*, Norwich Castle Museum & Art Gallery, Norwich
Ripe for Picking Fruits and Flowers, Jim Kempner Fine Art, New York
Summer Exhibition, Stedelijk Museum, Amsterdam
Summer Exhibition 2005, Royal Academy, London
London Calling. Y[oung] B[ritish] A[rtists] Criss-Crossed, Galleri Kaare Berntsen, Oslo
Blumenstück Künstlers Glück, Museum Morsbroich Leverkusen, Leverkusen
The Body. Art & Science, National Museum, Stockholm
Contemporary Photography and the Garden — Deceits & Fantasies, The Middlebury College Museum of Art, Middlebury /The Parrish Art Museum, New York

2004 *Slimvolume 2004*, Redux, London
The Flower As Image: From Monet to Jeff Koons, Louisiana Museum, Humlebæk
Gwangju Biennale 13th Tallinn Print Triennial, Korea
Lille Expo, Lille
Garden of Eden, Helsinki City Art Museum, Helsinki
The Garden of Delights, Galería Guereta, Madrid
Flowers Observed. Flowers Transformed, The Warhol Museum, Pittsburgh
Art of the Garden, Tate Britain, London / Ulster Museum, Belfast / Manchester Art Gallery, Manchester
Secrets of the '90s, Museum voor Moderne Kunst Arnhem, Arnhem
Flowers, Mary Boone Gallery, New York
Ideale e Realtà, Galleria d'Arte Moderna di Bologna, Bologna

2003 *Fourth Plinth Proposal*, National Gallery, London
FRESH: Contemporary British Artists in Print, Edinburgh Printmakers, Edinburgh
Statements 7, 50th Venice Biennale, Venice
Decembristerne, Gallery Faurschou, Copenhagen
Independence, South London Gallery, London
Genomic Issues, Graduate Centre Art Gallery, New York
Bull's Eye; Works from the Astrup Fearnley Collection, Arken Museum of Modern Art, Arken
UnNaturally, Contemporary Art Museum, University of South Florida, Tampa / Kansas City Art Institute, Kansas City / Fisher Gallery, University of Southern California, Los Angeles / Copia: The American Center for Wine, Food and the Arts, Napa / Lowe Art Museum, University of Miami, Coral Gables

2002 *Face Off*, Kettle's Yard, Cambridge
The Nude In Twentieth Century Art, Kunsthalle in Emden, Emden
Rapture: Art's Seduction by Fashion Since 1970, Barbican Gallery, London
Thinking Big: Concepts for 21st Century British Sculpture, Peggy Guggenheim Collection, Venice
The Rowan Collection. Contemporary British & Irish Art, Irish Museum on Modern Art, Dublin
Life is Beautiful, Laing Art Gallery, Newcastle
In the Freud Museum, Freud Museum, London
Iconoclash. Image Wars in Science, Religion and Art, Center for Art and Media, Karlsruhe
Second Skin. Historical Life Casting and Contemporary Sculpture, Henry Moore Institute, Leeds

2001 *Sacred and Profane*, Mappin Gallery, Sheffield
Printers Inc., The Gallery, Stratford-upon-Avon
Summer Exhibition 2001, Royal Academy of Arts, London
Ohne Zögern: Die Sammlung Olbricht Teil 2. Without Hesitation, Gesellschartf für Aktuelle Kunst & Neues Museum Weserburg, Bremen

Metamorphosis and Cloning, Musée d'art Contemporaine de Montréal, Quebec
/Arts, The Lux, London
London Nomad, Cairo Biennale, Cairo
Mind the Gap, Wetterling Gallery, Stockholm
Give & Take, Victoria and Albert Museum, London
Heads and Hands, Decatur House Museum, Washington

2000 *Wellcome Wing*, The Science Museum, London
Spectacular Bodies: The Art and Science of the Human Body from Leonardo to Now, Hayward Gallery, London
Conversation, Milton Keynes Art Gallery, Milton Keynes
Out There, White Cube?, London
Psycho, Anne Faggionato, London

1999 *Skin*, Deste Foundation Centre for Contemporary Art, Athens
Something Warm and Fuzzy, Des Moines Art Center, Des Moines
Into the Light. Photographic Printing Out of the Darkroom, The Royal Photographic Society, Bath
Officina Europa, Galleria d'Arte Moderna di Bologna, Bologna
Now It's My Turn to Scream. Works by Contemporary British Artists from the Logan Collection, Haines Gallery, San Francisco
Presence, Tate Liverpool, Liverpool
Spaced Out: Late 1990s Works from Vicki and Kent Logan Collection, The CCA Institute, California
As Above, So Below : The Body's Equal Parts, Fabric Workshop, Philidelphia
Physical Evidence, Kettle's Yard, Cambridge

1998 *Family*, Inverleith House, Royal Botanic Garden, Edinburgh
Group exhibition, Galleri Faurschou, Copenhagen
Hope (Sufferance), Sun and Doves Gallery, London
The Colony Room 50th Anniversary Art Exhibition, A22 Projects, London
A Portrait of Our Times: An Introduction to the Logan Collection, San Francisco Museum of Modern Art, San Francisco
UK Maximum Diversity, Galerie Krinzinger, Benger Fabrik Bregenz, Bregenz
Sam Taylor-Wood, Tracey Emin, Gillian Wearing, Marc Quinn, Galerija Dante Marino Cettina, Umag
Inner Self, Mitchell-Innes & Nash, New York

1997 *The Quick and the Dead : Artists and Anatomy*, Royal College of Art, London / Mead Gallery, University of Warwick, Warwick / City Art Gallery, Leeds
Sensation, Royal Academy of Arts, London / Hamburger Bahnhof, Berlin / Brooklyn Museum of Art, New York
The Body, The Art Gallery of New South Wales, Sydney
Follow Me, Kunstverein Kehdingen, Freiburg
A Ilha do Tesouro, Fundaçao Calouste Gulbenkian, Lisbon

1996 *Thinking Print. Books to Billboards 1980–95*, Museum of Modern Art, New York
Hybrid, De Appel, Amsterdam
Feed and Greed, MAK, Vienna
Works on Paper, Irish Museum of Modern Art, Dublin
Happy End, Kunsthalle, Dusseldorf

1995 *Time Machine*, Musee Egizio, Turin
Faith, Hope, Charity, Kunsthalle, Vienna
Contemporary British Art in Print, Scottish Museum of Modern Art, Edinburgh
Ripple Across the Water, Minato Prefecture and Shibuya Prefecture, Tokyo

1994 *Life is too Much*, Galerie des Archives, Paris
Time Machine, British Museum, London

1993 *Prospect '93*, Frankfurt
Sonsbeek '93, Arnhem
Art Cologne, (Saatchi Collection), Cologne
Real, Vienna Secession, Vienna
Restaurant, Marc Jancou, Paris
Young British Artists II, Saatchi Collection, London

1992 *Sydney Biennial*, Sydney
London Portfolio, Karsten Schubert, London
Strange Developments, Anthony d'Offay Gallery, London
British Art, Barbara Gladstone Gallery, New York

1991 *Modern Masters*, Grob Gallery, London

1990 *Group Show*, Grob Gallery, London
Hands, Grob Gallery, London

Other projects

2005 Screening of film *Marc Quinn*, The Prince's Drawing School, London, 9 March
Artists On Film Screening: Marc Quinn South Bank Show 2000 followed by Q&A with Gerry Fox & Marc Quinn, National Portrait Gallery, London 27 October.

Talks

2005 BP Artist's Talk: *Marc Quinn in conversation with Tim Marlow*, 11 October, Tate Britain, London

Awards

Fourth Plinth Commission for Trafalgar Square, London, 2004
The Royal Academy of Arts Charles Wollaston Award, 2001

Public Collections

Arario Gallery, Korea
Arts Council Collection, London
Art Gallery Museum (Royal Pump Rooms at the Parade), Leamington Spa
Astrup Fearnley Moderne Kunst, Oslo
British Museum, London
Brooklyn Museum of Art, New York
Caldic Collection, Rotterdam
Deutsche Bank, London
Denver Art Museum, Denver
Germentes Museum, Arnhem
Guggenheim Museum, New York
Kröller Müller Museum, Otterlo
National Portrait Gallery, London
Marx Collection, Berlin
Metropolitan Museum, New York
Montreal Museum of Modern Art, Montreal
Museum of Modern Art, New York
Phoenix Art Museum, Phoenix
Pompidou Centre, Paris
Saatchi Collection, London
Sammlung Essl, Klosterneuburg
San Francisco Museum of Modern Art, San Francisco
Science Museum, London
Sheffield Galleries, Sheffield
Stedlijk Museum, Amsterdam
Tate Gallery, London

Thanks to the Fourth Plinth Committee and their chair, Sandy Nairne, Ken Livingstone, Mayor of London, Andrea Schlieker, the curator of the project, Justine Simmons and Jacqueline Rose from the GLA

In Italy, Umberto Ronchieri of E. Ronchieri marmi Franco Cervietti, Raffaella, Pievotti, Italo Lenzoni

Jay Jopling and White Cube, Honey Luard, Alexandra Bradley and Daniela Gareh

Mary Boone

At Marc Quinn Studio, Algela Gilligan, Melisa Digby-Bell and Alexi Williams

Chris Nash, Gaby Nash and Noel Condon at Arch Bronze foundry

Alison Lapper and Parys, Peter Hull

Georgia, Tiger and Lucas.

First Edition published 2006 by SteidlMACK

Production and printing by Steidl

SteidlMACK Düstere Str. 4 D–37073 Göttingen Germany
Phone + 49 551 49 60 60 Fax + 49 551 49 60 649
Mail@steidl.de www.steidl.de www.steidlville.com
ISBN 3–86521–240–9
ISBN 13: 978-3–86521–240–5